Nature, Essence and Anarchy

Paul Cudenec

Winter Oak Press, Sussex, England, 2016

winteroak.org.uk

ISBN: 978-0-9576566-8-0

*"To the future or to the past, to a time when
thought is free, when men are different from one
another and do not live alone – to a time when
truth exists and what is done cannot be undone.
From the age of uniformity, from the age of
solitude, from the age of Big Brother, from the age
of double-think – greetings!"*

George Orwell, *1984*

CONTENTS

PREFACE

At a time when the very future of our species and of planetary life is at threat from the unchecked growth of the industrial capitalist cancer, the need for a powerful and coherent resistance can hardly be disputed. One of the effects of this disease, however, has been a thought-paralysis which renders any authentic and holistic anti-capitalist philosophy difficult to conceive and communicate. This is not by chance, of course – it is by disabling our intellectual immune system that the illness has been able to take and maintain control over us.

As well as fighting capitalism in a physical and day-to-day sense, we need to fight it in our heads and in our hearts by rooting our thinking in a healthy intellectual soil beyond the mental toxicity of its philosophically polluted wastelands. However, to expound a world-view that stands outside the received wisdom of contemporary industrial rigidities is far from simple when you have to communicate using a language which has been remodelled to reflect the requirements of capitalist modernity and when you are addressing a public whose deepest assumptions are those ingrained by the very system you seek to challenge.

In previous books, namely *The Anarchist Revelation, The Stifled Soul of Humankind* and *Forms of Freedom,* I have attempted to set out one overall argument that runs throughout the length of the book, developing sequentially from one chapter to the next. This is not the case here. Instead, you will find a series of separate essays, addressing similar issues from different angles. Each essay is like a cross-section of the overarching critique I am trying to present, through which a particular seam of analysis is revealed. One practical advantage of this format is that the reader can safely feel free to read the chapters in any order that happens to appeal. I also hope that the intersections and parallels between the various essays, as well as the spaces between them, will help stimulate the reader's thinking in ways that are not possible within a single linear thread.

The first essay, *Natural anarchy*, begins with an echoing of Guy Debord's condemnation of the world of artifice in which we live. I describe how, in order to hide its own falsity, capitalism denies that humanity belongs to a holistic natural world and also denies the very possibility of authenticity. I discuss the way that, despite Peter Kropotkin's work in describing the evolutionary importance of mutual aid and solidarity for all species, including humanity, many anarchists remain strangely suspicious of the idea of "nature". Widespread misuse of the word, and the effects on our thinking of the industrial society surrounding us, make it difficult to reclaim the term and overcome our separation. I look at the nature-based philosophy of the 16th century physician Paracelsus and suggest that we might rediscover authenticity by feeling within ourselves what he termed the *Spiritus Mundi*, the vital energy of the universe.

The second essay, *Denying reality: from nominalism to newthink*, explores the way in which contemporary society has a problem with objective reality. George Orwell warned about this in his novel *1984*, in which the Big Brother state insists that everything exists only in the human mind. I argue that this fallacy dates back to medieval nominalism, when traditional "universals" were redefined as merely words describing human-invented categories. Postmodernists and postanarchists today extend this approach to deny the validity of concepts like essence. Everything is said to be a construct. Subjective language is confused with objective reality. Anything outside industrial capitalist reality is denied legitimacy, trapping us within the dominant mindset.

In *When negative is positive*, I stress that the

anarchist desire to destroy capitalist society cannot be regarded as negative. For one thing, it aims to clear the way for a better world. But it also arises from a belief, as voiced by Rudolf Rocker and Noam Chomsky amongst others, that an anarchist society is always possible and that humans have the capacity to live harmoniously as a social organism. This capacity, which is innately present in the human mind but not always activated, reflects the overall tendency of the universe to take on a coherent structure. Conflict arises when the innate structures of the human mind meet an external world which does not allow them to fulfil their potential. As Otto Gross explains, some individuals give way and adapt to circumstances, while others rebel. A hatred of corrupt and unnatural society is founded on a positive vision of how things are *meant* to be.

Essence and empowerment begins by suggesting that modern life maintains us in a state of metaphysical sensory deprivation. If we wish to discover our core reality we need to look deep within ourselves. "Know Thyself" is a maxim dating back to at least Ancient Greek times and still central to contemporary paganism. The descent into the unconscious to find the Self, as invoked by anarchist Gustav Landauer for instance, is a reconnection to the organic universe described by Plato and Plotinus and also by the Sufi tradition. Understanding the individual as an aspect of a greater collective entity does not deny individual freedom, but rather removes the limits imposed upon it by our separation and reveals an empowering and anarchic truth, always regarded as a dangerous heresy by authority.

In *Naturaphobia and the industrial-capitalist death cult* I insist that humankind's belonging to the living flesh of our planet is an essential reality of our innermost nature and will always resurface in our spirit. The industrial system finds ingenious ways of blocking and diverting our awareness of this. It claims that the "progress" of its technologies equates to an upward path for humanity. Some on the left have fallen into the trap of equating individual freedom with the artificiality of industrial capitalism and of thus condemning "naturalism" and "essentialism" as reactionary. Transhumanism is an extreme example of this trend. Its nature-hating naturaphobia and life-denying vitaphobia are combined with a denial of the polluting and destructive realities behind its sanitised industrial-capitalist image of the future.

The starting point of *The eye of the heart* is that escaping the capitalist mindset is like digging a tunnel out of a prison camp. We need to go far enough and deep enough to go beyond its perimeter fences. Anarchists often fall short of understanding that industrial society is inherently capitalist and swallow the lie of "progress". Mahatma Gandhi understood the need to oppose industrialism and rediscover simple village life, the natural harmony of *Sanatan Dharma*. Traditional culture has always been an obstacle to capitalism and has been systematically eradicated across the world. I further join E.F. Schumacher and Ranchor Prime in calling for humankind to draw on our ancient spiritual wisdom so we can deepen our opposition to capitalism. We must access the "eye of the heart" to better understand multi-faceted reality. We need a metaphysical dimension to our revolt to allow us to pass completely outside the concrete confines of modern industrialist dogma.

In the final and longest piece, *Necessary subjectivity*, I write that the well-known phrase "think globally, act locally" translates on a philosophical level as "think objectively, act subjectively". If, like Plato and Plotinus, we define The Universe as all-inclusive, it necessarily includes abstracts as well as objects – numbers, dimensions, capacities and possibilities. We can never know the objective reality of this Universe, but we can know that this objective reality must exist and that it includes abstracts. Each of us has an abstract essence, which is a potential rather than a limit:

the butterfly essence, for instance, exists even within a caterpillar which is eaten by a bird before this physical stage is realised. The specific realities of our subjective existence must always provisionally limit our core essence as aspects of The Universe, of which we should be metaphysically aware. But this limiting is also the only way in which The Universe can manifest itself in physical form. The same applies to time. We can only experience time through the necessary subjectivity of our living, just as a needle must follow the groove of a vinyl record. But the whole piece of music is always contained in the record, in the same way as all time must be contained within a Universe which contains everything. Our subjective presence-in-the-present means we do not just observe events unfolding, but participate in the process. We are part of the self-shaping of The Universe, with all the responsibility that this implies.

All in all, these essays are perhaps best imagined as a handful of philosophical stones hurled from within a crowd of protesters towards the massed ranks of riot cops who have surrounded them. They are all slightly different in form and trajectory, but essentially they are all coming from the same place and aimed at the same opposition. I can only hope that one or two of my ideological lumps of rock will hit their intended targets and help break open the restricting encirclement of our thinking by the life-denying cyborgs of the industrial-capitalist Thought Police.

2016

1

NATURAL ANARCHY

The capitalist world in which we live is a world of artifice. Everything about it is fake, from the cancer-causing industrial food that rolls off its factory conveyor belts to the so-called "needs" that it claims to answer. As Guy Debord writes at the beginning of *The Society of the Spectacle*: "The whole life of those societies in which modern conditions of production prevail presents itself as an immense accumulation of spectacles. All that once was directly lived has become mere representation".[1] It is a world where "the commodity contemplates itself in a world of its own making",[2] a world of "the superficial reign of images".[3] Its version of the past is as fake as its vision of the future, its democracy as much a manipulative illusion as the constant threats conjured up by its propaganda to keep us in our place. Its very idea of normality is fake: its alienated individuals; its weekly rhythms of paid labour and consumption; its imposed concepts of land "ownership", "legitimate authority", "nationality".

Moreover, this capitalist world reduces everything to its own shallow terms, cannot admit that there is anything beyond the four thin walls of its own empty, sterile, valueless universe. There can be no meaning in the world, because meaning has no place in its thinking. There can be no authenticity, because the very existence of that term would throw into sharp relief its own fundamental *inauthenticity*. For the constructed capitalist world, everything else has *also* been constructed. Aware on some level of its own fundamental falsity, it defends itself by projecting that falsity on to everything else that exists, in order to level the playing field and create a theoretical realm in which its own artifice no longer stands out as aberrant, alien, toxic. It becomes impossible to accuse capitalism, *in particular*, of being fake if you accept its big lie that everything, *in general*, is fake, and that there is no such thing as truth, meaning, origin, essence and nature.

But what if we reject that lie? What if we dare to look beyond the material and philosophical artifice with which have been surrounded since birth and search for something *real* on which to base our understanding? Here we will have stepped beyond the perimeter fence of the possibilities as dictated to us by the dominant system of all-embracing mendacity. We will be wandering in forests of thought that are not marked on the street-maps of modernity, encountering outlaws and thought-criminals regarded as dangerous by our mind-masters, taking paths that lead us far beyond the limits of the world as laid out for us by their systems of domination.

The very first reality we encounter, on emerging from the capitalist world of falsity, is that we, as human beings, are in fact part of nature. This is a truth that has been denied to us, in the West, for centuries – initially by the religious form previously taken by the tyranny that still stifles us today.[4] "Separation is the alpha and omega of the spectacle",[5] writes Debord and by reclaiming that primal sense of belonging to our world we shatter that separation, free ourselves from the mirrored cage of self-referential human intellectuality.

Our understanding begins with the knowledge of what we are in our flesh, by breathing and feeling the raw actuality of our own physical presence. As John Zerzan sets out in *Why Hope? The Stand Against Civilization*: "This is the age of disembodiment, when our sense of separateness from the Earth grows and we are meant to forget our animality. But we are animals and we co-evolved, like all animals, in rapport with other bodily forms and aspects of the world".[6]

For all the layers of self-deception we have built up around us, we cannot alter the fact that "we are still animals on the planet, with all its original messages waiting in our being".[7] If we are to ever forge a new future completely free of the alienating lies of the industrial capitalist spectacle, we will need to find roots for our thinking that predate our contemporary separation. Ancient wisdom, folk culture, myth and lore can all feed into our understanding of who and what we are, so that we can fashion a sense of grounded freedom emerging from our inseparability from the natural world to which we owe our physical being. There are also individual thinkers who carry seeds of that awareness to us and whose work needs to be reappraised, demarginalised and used to help build our new/old metaphysics of liberation.

One of these is Aureolus Theophrastus Bombastus von Hohenheim (1493-1541), better known as Paracelsus. The wandering Swiss-born polymath, philosopher and physician is often remembered today as one of the early precursors of modern medicine. But he in fact represents a late and creative flowering of an ancient way of thinking that was to be crushed under the iron wheels of industrial capitalism in the centuries to come. His philosophy is based on a holistic concept of living nature. He declares: "Nature, made of the Universe, is one and its origin can only be the eternal Unity. It is a vast organism in which natural things harmonise and sympathise between themselves".[8] Animating all this is "the vital energy of the Universe (*Spiritus Mundi*)",[9] a "fundamental, invisible, vital, vitalising force".[10]

Lucien Braun summarises Paracelsus's idea of nature thus: "It is indeed everything that we see before our eyes: trees, minerals, animals, diseases, birth, death... But what it gives us is always something else as well: the manifestation of a 'deeper' reality – although for the time being we cannot define this depth more clearly. Nature is simultaneously visible and invisible: visible in form, invisible in power – but the two aspects are intimately bound".[11] He explains how, for Paracelsus, "the Great World shines in every being, in every plant, in every mineral".[12] It does so by means of a subsidiary principle, a star or *Gestirn*, which lies behind their particular physical form. A specific seed grows into a specific tree because of this inner essence manifesting itself.

"It's advisable, therefore, not to remain on the superficial level of things, or to look merely at the determination of forms. On the contrary, we should never consider a visible determination without at the same time considering the agency presupposed by this determination, in other words the invisible and secret force behind the principle of its manifestation. This is how we must read nature, everywhere: in the intimate unity of the visible and the invisible".[13]

Even when we are engaged in philosophy, we cannot leave the realm of a nature which is, after all, universal and all-embracing. Nature is certainly the *object* of Paracelsus's enquiries: "What is philosophy if not the discovery of invisible nature?",[14] he asks. But, at the same time, it is also their *subject*. The Paracelsian concept of the philosopher has nothing in common with the model of the modern scientist, an outside observer of all that takes place in the separated realm he is studying. "According to Paracelsus, the real philosopher no longer belongs to himself, but serves nature", writes Patrick Rivière.[15] More than serving nature, he *is* nature, serving itself. The philosopher and his philosophy are *both part of the self-revealing of nature.*

Paracelsus spent his life speaking out against dogmatism, against the fixed orthodoxy of Medieval medicine, against the exploitation of the poor: "in short", says Braun, "against everything which he regarded as artifice or convention".[16] It is, therefore, nothing less than tragic that the breadth of his thinking, the opening-out of the human spirit that he represented, was to be closed down again by new waves of artifice and convention, new modern versions of dogmatism and orthodoxy.

The rationalism of the Enlightenment brought with it all the scientific, positivist thinking that fitted so well with the pragmatic realities of the capitalists' Industrial Revolution. There was no more place for open-ended thinking, for the embracing of paradox, for the awareness that the mysteries of the universe must ultimately lie beyond the complete grasp of human beings. The multi-dimensionality of *wisdom* was replaced by the one-dimensionality of mere *knowledge* and "knowledge is truth externalised, displaced, thrown off centre. It is, for Paracelsus, something like sin".[17]

Nature as seen by Paracelsus was not something that could readily be flattened out into a scientific theory or mathematical equation. As Braun says: "Nature, despite all the attempts at interpreting it, cannot be tied down (*capitur*): it instantly eludes all concept. It bursts the banks of language. And Paracelsus's work can only be an impossible attempt to express with words (nearly 8,000 pages of them!) something which has always been thought by its author to stretch beyond the possibilities of plain logic".[18]

The new industrial society needed a new definition of nature that could be expressed in its own restricted scientific language and which would "correspond with the new consciousness that man (now bourgeois) had of himself".[19] Thus, in the centuries following Paracelsus's death, we see the ideological construction of "a nature which was inert (and thus artless, lifeless), which was conceived in mechanical terms and was therefore open to mechanisation and boundless manipulation".[20]

A highly significant part of this process was the creation in the 19th century of a theory of evolution which fitted in perfectly with all the assumptions of imperialistic industrial capitalism. The message of Charles Darwin's *On the Origin of Species*, published in 1859, was taken to be that the domination of the poor by the rich, of workers by bosses, of indigenous people by Europeans, was all perfectly "natural". Indeed, it was claimed, this domination was essential for evolution – if the economically and physically unfit were allowed to thrive and breed, the progress of humanity would be thrown into reverse.

The obvious response from socialists and anarchists, as Renaud Garcia states, was to "develop a critique of the 'naturalist' illusion, in other words the idea according to which we ascertain what we can justifiably expect from human societies on the basis of a human essence possessing a certain number of immutable characteristics".[21] But then anarchist scientist Peter Kropotkin came up with a new interpretation of the political implications of evolutionary theory. He showed that the struggle between individuals was an inadequate description of the workings of nature and that co-operative mutual aid was a much more important factor among all species, including humankind.

Kropotkin wrote in *Mutual Aid*, first published in 1902: "'Don't compete! – competition is always injurious to the species and you have plenty of resources to avoid it!' That is the *tendency* of nature, not always realized in full, but always present. That is the watchword that comes to us from the bush, the forest, the river, the ocean. 'Therefore combine – practise mutual aid! That is the surest means for giving to each and to all the greatest safety, the best guarantee of existence and progress, bodily, intellectual, and moral'. That is what Nature teaches us; and that is what all those animals which have attained the highest position in their respective classes have done".[22]

In simple terms, he was saying that anarchism is natural – that, left to their own devices, people and other animals tend to co-operate with others for their collective benefit. Kropotkin was essentially echoing, in the scientific language of his time, Paracelsus's vision of nature as "a vast organism in which natural things harmonise and sympathise between themselves".

The view of nature as violently competitive

has always been used as the pretext for the existence of a state in order to keep all the dreadful chaos under control. Demolishing this *fake* idea of "nature" and replacing it with an understanding of complex organic harmony would therefore seem to be central to the anarchist project. As Theodore Roszak has noted: "Anarchism has always been, uniquely, a politics swayed by organic sensibility; it is born of a concern for the health of cellular structure in society and a confidence in spontaneous self-regulation".[23]

Kropotkin's ideological intervention totally undermined the industrial capitalist claim that its inhuman and exploitative system was merely evolution in practice – and thus, also, *removed the need for anti-capitalists to distance themselves from any notion of nature.* But while Kropotkin is still respected and quoted today, the primary relevance of his response to the reactionary Darwinists often seems to have been overlooked or misunderstood. The anarchic quality of nature, and thus the naturalness of anarchy, has not taken the central place in anarchist ideology that might have been expected. Under the pervasive influence of Enlightenment rationalism and its industrialist intellectual offshoots (including Marxism), many anarchists have kept the idea of nature at arm's length.[24] For all Kropotkin's work, ideas of "naturalness" continue to be associated with reactionary positions and it is often held that there is no continuity between the natural world and human society. Ultimately, this amounts to a claim that human beings are somehow outside of nature altogether, as if we had dropped on to this planet from outer space. This is a metaphysical separation of "man" from "beast" shared with Christian dogma, a ridiculous human vanity that blinds us to the truth that for all our idiosyncrasies we remain animals, we remain part of nature.

Braun writes that when Paracelsus ponders what is philosophy "if not the discovery of invisible nature", he goes on to declare that "all philosophy which deviates from that goal is pseudo-philosophy (*Schaumphilosophie*) and is like fungus growing on a tree and remaining outside it".[25] Any philosophy which is based on a denial of our belonging to nature is based on a lie. Any further ideas constructed on that mendacious foundation can have no truthful solidity. Since Paracelsus's day, whole layers of *Schaumphilosophie* have accumulated in the modern mind, creating the artifice of Debord's all-suffocating spectacle. These layers of falsity make it almost impossible to express truths that are denied by the spectacle. This is hardly surprising as that is the whole *raison d'être* of the falsity – it is intellectual cover for industrial capitalism, a fake "reality" in which that spectacle makes sense and anything outside of that spectacle makes no sense at all.

We have now reached a layer of falsity in which it has become possible not simply to claim that nature is something apart from humankind but to claim that nature does not exist at all and is merely a *construct* of humankind. Of course, human *definitions* of nature are all constructs. And the idea that we should or can *define* nature in the first place is the product of narrowed-down rationalist thinking. But the falsity of *definitions* of "nature" does not mean that nature itself does not exist! The fact that nature *can never be defined* does not mean that it *does not exist*. Indeed, we might almost say that its indefinable character is part of its (non-)definition. It simply cannot be reduced to mere words.

The inability to distinguish between words and reality is a key feature of contemporary *Schaumphilosophie*. It arises from the same human hubris that imagines us to be outside nature, *superior* to the rest of life on the planet. Our self-indulgent vanity has reached a level at which we imagine that the human words which we use *actually create physical reality* and that by exposing these words as mere words, we also somehow affect or undermine the physical reality they were intended to describe.[26] Humans invent a word called "nature" to describe the world to which they belong and then declare that this was just a word they invented and that therefore they do not belong to the world at all! This is an advanced stage of sophisticated fakery – *fabricating a lie and then pointing to its falsity in order to disallow the truth that it had falsely purported to designate.*

All of this is the end result of a human subjectivity that has gone far beyond the stage necessary for us to conduct our subjective individual lives[27] and has turned into an egocentric denial of external objective reality. Discussing Paracelsus's understanding of a universe that reveals itself in us, Braun comments: "It is clear that we find ourselves here at complete odds with everything that would be taught to us, in the centuries to come, by the philosophies of the subject which would try to explain the world on the basis of the capacities and categories of the subject! There, the world would become an image of myself. Here, it's the World which tries to know itself and find its fulfilment through the human being".[28]

Ultra-subjectivism on a philosophical level translates to ultra-individualism on a social level and the same barriers to contemporary understanding of Paracelsus also block understanding of anarchist thinking. The co-operative nature described by Kropotkin is the foundation stone of human society – society as it *should* be, in any case. But in a world that sees only atomised individuals creating their own subjective realities, what place is there for this collective level of human life, so important for socialist and anarchist theory? In our capitalist world of separation, any authentic communal belonging has to be destroyed so that each isolated individual has to turn to the system for their sense of identity, which is sold back to them in fake form as part of a lifelong process of exploitation based on dispossession.

The psychological separation of humanity from nature is part of the same phenomenon as our separation from each other in our industrial capitalist cities. The anarchist aim of reforging those social bonds, creating solidarity and mutual aid, therefore goes hand in hand with the aim of reforging our bonds with nature. Reversal of separation, reversal of isolation, reversal of exploitation, reversal of ultra-individualism, reversal of ultra-subjectivism, reversal of capitalism, reversal of industrialism – these are not so much intersecting struggles as facets of one and the same effort.

The immediate task at hand is the peeling away of all the layers of lies, of *Schaumphilosophie,* that have accumulated over the centuries. However, this is incredibly difficult, since we all live entirely within the spectacle of lies that is deceiving us. Insights that come from somewhere outside that paradigm make no sense to someone whose understanding of the world is entirely contained within the fake assumptions it harbours. The idea that we could live without a state seems laughably naïve to someone who has been conditioned to believe that authority exists to protect us, not to enslave us, that we *need* rulers in order to stop society descending into the chaotic violence that would inevitably result if we were left to our own devices. The idea that we could live happily without industrial infrastructure seems ridiculous to someone whose whole life has been led within that system, who associates the search for food with visits to the supermarket and companionship with electronic communication. The idea that we, as human beings, are part of nature seems absurd and dangerous to someone who has learnt to regard nature as either an external non-human reality, a romanticised fantasy or a kind of violent brute force that has constantly to be repressed by civilized human society.

It is not just our intellectual environment that determines these reactions, but the physical one, too. If we live in an urban, industrialised outer world then our inner world risks being limited to the shallowness of all that is urban and industrialised. Braun writes that Paracelsus's ideas make no sense in the context of modern surrounds which "impoverish us to our very depths by depriving us of real images, by filling our vision with right angles and machines, in other words with ontologically shallow products spawned by a rationalism of representation. We are far from the sights which would have sparked Paracelsus's imagination in the depths of the Swiss forests, teeming with forms and beings, and which would have spoken to him in quite a different way than do the concreted spaces of today".[29]

If our everyday experience is of traffic jams, shopping malls and office blocks, if our minds are constantly filled with images of consumerism, domination and war, how are we to see the world as "a vast organism in which natural things harmonise and sympathise between themselves"? The answer is in our imagination. As anarchists have long understood, another world is always possible and will flourish in our collective mind long before it becomes a physical reality. We need to *imagine* ourselves out of the suffocating confines of industrial capitalism, leaping over all the barriers of lies that it has erected around us. We need to *dream* ourselves into a state of authenticity – to allow *nature to dream itself into the core of our inner being.* "Freedom for Paracelsus is anything but the arbitrary will of the subject," says Braun. "It is not defined on the basis of the subject, of the will of the subject.

Instead, it's an act of letting-be, letting nature illuminate itself in us".[30]

We need to reach out beyond the cardboard cut-out words which seek to define, reduce and destroy reality; we need to feel within ourselves the *Spiritus Mundi,* the vital energy of the universe. This is how we can find freedom, the natural freedom of anarchy which arises from intertwined individuality and collectivity, unaffected by the metaphysical separation that is the "alpha and omega of the spectacle". And if this authenticity is hidden from us by an ultra-individualism and ultra-subjectivity that has enclosed the whole terrain of modern industrialised thinking, then we will have to tear down the barriers of that false mindset and plant a holistic philosophy for the future in the living soil of our neglected metaphysical past.

1. Guy Debord, *La société du spectacle* (Paris: Gallimard, 1992), 1, p. 3.

2. Debord, 53, p. 31.

3. Debord, 199, p. 152.

4. Paul Cudenec, *The Stifled Soul of Humankind* (Sussex: Winter Oak Press, 2014).

5. Debord, 25, p. 13.

6. John Zerzan, *Why Hope? The Stand Against Civilization* (Port Townsend, WA: Feral House, 2015), p. 97.

7. Zerzan, p. 106.

8. Paracelsus, cit. Patrick Rivière, *Paracelse: medicin-alchimiste, "philosophe par le feu"* (Paris: Éditions de Vecchi, 2008), p. 97.

9. Rivière, p. 58.

10. Roland Edighoffer, *Préface,* in Lucien Braun, *Paracelse* (Paris-Geneva: Éditions Slatkine, 1995) p. x.

11. Braun p. 36.

12. Braun pp.158-59.

13. Braun, p. 37.

14. Paracelsus, *Sämtliche Werke,* VIII, 71, cit. Braun p. 51.

15. Rivière, p. 91.

16. Braun, p. 11.

17. Braun p. 34.

18. Braun p. 31.

19. Braun p. 43.

20. Ibid.

21. Renaud Garcia, *La nature de l'entraide: Pierre Kropotkine et les fondements biologiques de l'anarchisme* (Lyon: ENS Éditions, 2015), p. 16.

22. Peter Kropotkin, *Mutual Aid: A Factor of Evolution* (London: Freedom Press, 1993), p. 73.

23. Theodore Roszak, *Where the Wasteland Ends: Politics and Transcendence in Postindustrial Society* (New York: Doubleday, 1972), p. 424.

24. François Jarrige, for instance, tells how the *anarchisme naturien* which emerged in Paris and elsewhere in France at the end of the 19th century and start of the 20th century was attacked and sidelined both by Marxists and by elements within the anarchist movement itself and eventually

disappeared, only to re-emerge in the 21st century in the form of the anarchist wing of the contemporary *décroissance* (degrowth) movement. François Jarrige, *Gravelle, Zisly et les anarchistes naturiens contre la civilisation industrielle* (Neuvy-en-Champagne: Éditions le passager clandestin, *Les Précurseurs de la Décroissance* collection, 2016).

25. Braun p. 51.

26. See *2. Denying reality: from nominalism to newthink.*

27. See *7. Necessary subjectivity.*

28. Braun, pp. 157-58.

29. Braun, pp. 238-39.

30. Braun, pp. 45-46.

2

DENYING REALITY: FROM NOMINALISM TO *NEWTHINK*

You can tell a lot about the metaphysical health of a society from the philosophical questions it asks itself. In the case of our own culture, one of the best-known such questions is: "If a tree falls in a forest and no one is around to hear it, does it make a sound?" The answer is quite obviously "yes" and the question is ridiculous on more than one level. For one thing, it is blindly anthropocentric, assuming that the presence of a human being somehow makes a unique difference to the reality of sound. But even if the "no one" in the question includes the whole range of non-human living creatures that might have heard the hypothetical tree, the whole thing is still inherently absurd. The tree cannot fall silently. It will make a noise as it hits the ground, regardless of whether or not this is witnessed.

This so-called "philosophical puzzle" reflects a deep underlying problem with contemporary thinking, in that it potentially denies the existence of *objective reality*, suggesting that the crashing sound made by the tree may only become *real* if it is *subjectively experienced* by some "one". This denial of objective truth is identified as a dangerous delusion by George Orwell in his book *1984*. Although presented as a science-fiction warning of a totalitarian society to come, Orwell's classic novel is, of course, a commentary on mid-20th century realities, exaggerated and projected on to a fictional future. Thus the propaganda machineries of the *Ministry of Truth* are very much inspired by the author's personal experiences working for the BBC in London during the Second World War. Likewise with Orwell's astute observations on a more abstract philosophical level – he is warning us of the way things are heading.

In the novel, Ingsoc's Big Brother dictatorship has established near-complete control of the population not merely on a physical level, but on a psychological one too – it is able to manipulate the experience of those it dominates, by denying the possibility of any objective reality. "Not merely the validity of experience, but the very existence of external reality was tacitly denied by their philosophy. The heresy of heresies was common sense... If both the past and external world exist only in the mind, and if the mind itself is controllable – what then?"[1]

When O'Brien, the Inner Party stalwart, is torturing the novel's hero, Winston Smith, he tells him: "You believe that reality is something objective, external, existing in its own right... But I tell you, Winston, that reality is not external. Reality exists in the human mind, and nowhere else".[2] Later, he again stresses: "Nothing exists except through human consciousness".[3] Winston's struggle to keep a grip on objective reality, to know that two plus two makes four whatever the ideological demands of the Party, is a central theme of Orwell's novel. Early on in the story the character tells himself: "Truisms are true, hold on to that! The solid world exists, its laws do not change. Stones are hard, water is wet, objects unsupported fall towards the earth's centre".[4] Orwell has him conclude: "There was truth and there was untruth. And if you clung to the truth even against the whole world, you were not mad".[5]

But thanks to all the torture and brainwashing doled out by O'Brien and his comrades, Winston ends up becoming a defeated conformist *goodthinker* and deciding that this idea of objective truth was an obvious fallacy because "it presupposed that somewhere or other, outside oneself, there was a 'real' world where 'real' things happened. But how could there be such a world? What knowledge have we of anything, save through our own minds? All happenings are in the mind".[6] Having rid himself of the *oldthink* notion of objective truth, the way is clear for him to accept that two and two does indeed make five – or any other number that the Party demands.

There seems to be something very modern about this strange delusion that truth is brought into being by someone *thinking* it, that the sound of a tree falling is purely the result of someone *hearing* it, that the result of a mathematical process is whatever we *want* it to be. But I suspect that its origins can be traced back to the latter part of the Middle Ages and the emergence of nominalism. Nominalism, or the *via moderna* as it was known for a while, represented a challenge to the certainties of the original *oldthink* – or *via antiqua* – which had been inherited from classical Greek philosophy and before that from a *catena aurea* or golden chain of thought stretching back into remotest antiquity.

This traditional approach, known as realism at the time and today usually termed essentialism, holds that there is an essential reality behind the specifics that surround us in everyday life. This essential reality casts the shadows on the wall of the cave in Plato's famous philosophical tale. The prisoners mistake the moving shapes for actual reality in the same way that we might mistake temporary physical manifestations of essential reality for the real thing. The concept is most clearly imagined in terms of numbers. The number "three" exists in abstract form, without the need for the existence of three actual things. The possibility of there being three of something (or seven or nineteen) is always present. The numbers themselves can therefore be described as "existing" – or "subsisting" – on a level more abstract and less transient than that of physical reality. Likewise, the possibilities of "duration" in time or of "extension" in physical space clearly exist in the same way that mathematical concepts exist, even though they cannot be seen, touched, smelled or heard. The same was held to be true of terms such as "dark" or "light", "cold" or "hot" and so on – there was an idea that existed in a real but non-physical way, as a kind of necessary potentiality behind actual physical things.

The new thinking challenged the notion that these abstract "universals" actually existed as "things" on some level. Fourteenth century thinker William of Ockham said that all such categories were, instead, concepts formed in the human mind, while fully-fledged nominalists said these categories were just words – hence "nominalism", from *nomen*, the Latin for "name". The nominalists were not disputing the existence of objective reality as such, just the existence or subsistence of universals, which they regarded as categories which had merely been created in our heads. However, with historical hindsight, this was a significant step towards the human narcissism that was to characterise the centuries to come. We were starting to imagine certain intangible non-human aspects of the world around us as merely the *constructs* of human minds and language.

As humans were increasingly separated from the rest of nature by the industrialisation of society, the process was justified by the new ways of thinking. Thomas Hobbes (1588-1679) redefined the interconnected organic natural world as a brutal battlefield between selfish individual creatures, while John Locke (1632-1704) effectively denied that humans even formed part of nature, but claimed they were born with no innate qualities at all. This, of course, made them the entirely-malleable products of the specific human society into which they were born.

This industrial-scientific thinking, in the form of positivism, dominated European thought for centuries and paved the way for the massive social changes, termed "progress", which have created the world we find ourselves in today. If humans were not part of nature, it was simply there to be exploited for our own benefit. If human communities did not exist, but were just collections of individuals, there was no problem in destroying them.

Inevitably, though, there has been some reaction to the rigidity of this scientific-capitalist outlook (which also, unfortunately, infected supposedly oppositional philosophies such as socialism and anarchism[7]). Some of this reaction took the form of what Michael Löwy describes as "Romantic anti-capitalism"[8] and related currents of thought reclaiming the connection to the natural world denied by positivism. Another angle involved a deep analysis of the relationships and structures within human society, which revealed realities overlooked by over-simplistic economic and social analysis. This very much appealed to anarchists, whose broad critique of contemporary capitalist society had always reached down below the surface of economic life into the murky zone of all those assumptions and formulations which make up the system of domination. Gustav Landauer, for instance, had been pointing out as early as 1910 that: "The state is a social relationship; a certain way of people relating to one another. It can be destroyed by creating new social relationships; i.e., by people relating to one another differently".[9]

The criticism of mass society pioneered by the Frankfurt School and the Situationists was taken in interesting new directions by Michel Foucault and other postmodern thinkers. They identified hidden power structures embedded in society – within the mental health system, prisons, education, families and in gender definitions, for instance. In many ways this analysis sat well with anarchist thinking, in that it exposed and challenged means of social control that were not obvious on the "political" surface. Saul Newman, in his influential essay *The Politics of Postanarchism*, claims that postanarchism, which is part of this general trend, has performed "a salvage operation on classical anarchism" and broadened its philosophical horizons.[10]

But this approach also brought with it certain problems and in many instances served to undermine, rather than underwrite, left-wing criticism of capitalist society. This phenomenon is discussed in some detail by Renaud Garcia in his 2015 book *Le désert de la critique*.[11] Here he offers an invaluable analysis of the effect of the postmodern approach, particularly the intellectual impact of Foucaultian thought on anarchist and left-wing thinking. Of particular concern is the way that the postanarchists have continued where the post-medieval nominalists left off, in denying the existence of certain notions which were previously considered to be real. Foucault himself even used the label "nominalist" to describe his approach.[12] This deconstruction of reality goes well beyond the anarchist insight of denying fake concepts which are used to deceive and dominate – such as "property" or "law" or "nation". It questions the actual existence of any entity or structure which exploits and dominates us. In fact, the very context in which Foucault describes himself as a "nominalist" is in arguing that it is naive to think you can fight repressive external "power", since it *only* exists within inter-personal relationships.[13]

Newman likewise refutes the old-fashioned anarchist notion of there being "a subject whose natural human essence is repressed by power" and claims that "this form of subjectivity is actually an effect of power". He argues: "This subjectivity has been produced in such a way that it sees itself as having an essence that is repressed – so that its liberation is actually concomitant with its continued domination".[14] This comes dangerously close to a declaration that "Liberation is Domination" – a slogan worthy of being placed alongside "War is Peace" and "Slavery is Freedom" in the lexicon of Orwellian *goodthink*!

On a metaphysical level, postanarchists, like all postmodernists, deny that there is any essence behind anything in the world. Nothing in the human mind is innate and there is no such thing as human nature. The very idea of "humanity" as a universal concept is rejected. In his essay, Newman specifically opposes the notion of "a universal human essence with rational and moral characteristics"[15] which, as he notes, forms the basis of Kropotkin and Bakunin's anarchism. Indeed, not only do the postmodernists insist that universals do not exist, but they claim that the *very idea* of universals is part of the domination that we have to resist. Anything that smacks of "essentialism" is not only questionable, but dangerous.

It is at this point that the approach of the postanarchists starts to combine a version of nominalism with the manipulative dogmatism of Orwell's fictional Ingsoc totalitarianism. The meaning of terms is contaminated in order to make their continued usage unacceptable in *goodthinking* circles. Thus, for many contemporary left-wingers influenced by postmodernism, "essentialism" no longer indicates the metaphysical position held by Plotinus, Plato and generations of thinkers before them, but something more akin to a rigid social conservatism. For them, an "essentialist" is a reactionary who believes that each of us is born into a certain slot in society determined by our heredity, ethnicity, sex and so on. "Human nature" is likewise seen by Foucaultians as nothing but a *construct*, which is used to justify the narrow limits imposed on individual potential by a system of domination. This idea of "human nature" might dictate, for instance, that people should live in family units, pair off in monogamous heterosexual couples, restrict their own sense of identity to one deemed "natural" by that particular society.

From this postmodern point of view, the possibility of anything being "innate" to human beings is regarded as absurd, threatening and close to racism – it denies us the absolute freedom of constructing our own selves. The idea of something being "universal" is seen as an imposition from above, an attempt to eradicate diversity in the name of some all-embracing constructed standard. Even the concept of "humanity" itself is seen as being suspect by this school of thought and regarded as a plurality-denying device with which to bring people under a theoretical umbrella of domination.

However, these postanarchist definitions of essentialism, human nature or universality are nothing but caricatures, based on the narrowest and most reactionary usage of each term and imposing the worst-possible interpretation of the intent behind them (isn't it possible that someone who expands his or her personal vision to include the whole of humankind might be motivated by an open-hearted desire for *inclusion* rather than a manipulative urge for *repression*?). They are *straw man* definitions – deliberately inadequate representations of a certain point of view set up by an opponent for the sole purpose of being easily knocked down. As a result, the *real* philosophies behind these fake versions can no longer easily be distinguished and once the terms in question have successfully been contaminated, it becomes impossible to use them without immediately appearing to be expressing the completely unacceptable views with which they are now automatically associated. Orwell describes this linguistic blocking process in his novel: "*All mans are equal* was a possible Newspeak sentence, but only in the same sense in which *All men are redhaired* is a possible Oldspeak sentence. It did not contain a grammatical error, but it expressed a palpable untruth, i.e., that all men are of equal size, weight or strength. The concept of political equality no longer existed, and this secondary meaning had accordingly been purged out of the word *equal*".[16]

Contemporary "anti-naturalists" (to use Garcia's term) in fact pull off the impressive ideological gymnastic feat of endorsing right-wing definitions of words in order to dismiss as right-wing all those trying to use the words in different ways. Thus left-wing anarchist definitions of human nature (as intrinsically co-operative rather than competitive, as something potentially broad and diverse that has been stifled by the repressive limits of contemporary society) are ignored and replaced by narrow right-wing neo-Darwinist notions. Any use of the term "human nature" is thereafter interpreted as an endorsement of the right-wing version *adopted by the postmodernists themselves.* It becomes impossible to use "human nature" in a left-wing anarchist sense. You would think Kropotkin had never existed!

All of this manipulation is built on a misunderstanding of the relationship between human language and actual reality. It is simply not true to say that "nature", for instance, is *only* a word. It *is* a word, and thus capable of containing all sorts of meaning dictated by the cultural context in which it is used. But, like all words, it is *also* used to designate something beyond the word itself. Just because "nature" is a word does not mean it is not *also* a real thing. Sometimes, of course, words do not relate to something real at all. But the existence of a word certainly does not *preclude* the existence of a real thing, even though when a word describes something that is not empirically observable, the relationship between the word and the thing it designates becomes more difficult to grasp.

If I use the word "window", I am still using a mere word. The concept of "window" is large enough to include a variety of different kinds of window and one person's mental picture of what that window might look like will no doubt vary from another's. However, nobody would suggest that because "window" is *only* a word, there is no such thing as a window in *reality*. In fact we are talking about *two different phenomena* here, operating on two distinct levels. On the level of language there is the word "window" and on the level of reality there is the actual thing that is a window, in all its various specific manifestations. Supposing for some reason a society had misused the word "window" in some way – perhaps, for instance, by applying it solely to stained-glass windows of the kind used in churches. The word "window" as used by that society would therefore become suspect and loaded with an artificial and ecclesiastical restriction to its meaning. In the same way we might say that the word "nature" as used by 19th century right-wing neo-Darwinists also became suspect. But the suspect definition of the word "window" in that imaginary society would not mean that actual windows, as we know them, would have suddenly ceased to exist! There is no direct causal relationship here between the use of a specific word and the nature of objective reality. You can distort the meaning of the word "window" all you like, redefine it to mean "cabbage" if you choose, but the window next to me as I write these words will remain the same. Likewise, nature remains nature, regardless of how the mere word "nature" might be manipulated or misused. *Nature is not*

*in any way dependent on the human word
"nature" for its existence or essence.*

Postmodernists have fallen into the nominalist trap of believing that the reality of human language and thought – the subjective truth of human beings – is *more real than actual objective truth.* They mistake word for reality, shadow for object. This is not a question of whether or not we can adequately *understand* abstract realities, like "nature" or "universals". From our limited human perspective that may not be possible. But it is a mistake to imagine that something we cannot observe or define, or which we usually designate with a word that is loaded with our own limited subjective social assumptions, *consequently does not exist at all.* This mistake is like a small child playing "hide and seek" for the first time, who imagines that if he closes his eyes and thus cannot see his playmates, his playmates will not be able to see him either. This child has not grasped that his own subjective experience of reality is not the same as objective reality. This mistake is also like a contemporary philosopher who ponders long and hard over whether a tree crashing loudly to the earth in a forest can really be said to have made any sound, if this has not been subjectively experienced by a human being like him.

The political implications of this

metaphysical mess are worrying. We have now reached the sorry point where it seems that any mention of the *essence* behind something, or of anything remotely *universal*, sets the ideological alarm bells ringing. We are apparently expected to censor ourselves in advance by never uttering such terms and by deploying what Orwell terms *crimestop* – "the faculty of stopping short, as though by instinct, at the threshold of any dangerous thought".[17] This even now seems to apply to the classic anarchist argument, as put forward by Kropotkin, that *humanity* (stop!) is *innately* (stop!!) disposed to co-operation and mutual aid and thus could *naturally* (stop!!!) live perfectly well without state management.

In *1984*, one of the Party members developing Newspeak tells Winston Smith: "You think, I dare say, that our chief job is inventing new words. But not a bit of it! We're destroying words – scores of them, hundreds of them, every day".[18] He explains: "Don't you see that the whole aim of Newspeak is to narrow the range of thought? In the end we shall make thought-crime literally impossible, because there will be no words in which to express it... By 2050 – earlier, probably – all real knowledge of Oldspeak will have disappeared. The whole literature of the past will have been destroyed".[19]

In destroying the full metaphysical meaning of words like "essence", "nature" or "universal" by means of their straw man constructs, the conformists of contemporary *goodthink* are destroying our connection to reality. Because they ideologically object to everything beyond subjective individual experience, they are destroying, in particular, our connection to the reality that we human beings are *more than individuals*. They are destroying our understanding that our individual freedom and well-being are in fact dependent on a *collective* level of existence as part of a community, as part of a species and as part of nature as a whole. They are thus destroying our capacity to see what has been stolen from us by the alienation and separation of the industrial capitalist system and what it is that we must reclaim. "If one is to rule, and to continue ruling," declares Orwell's Emmanuel Goldstein, "one must be able to dislocate the sense of reality".[20] A philosophically dislocated anti-capitalist movement that has lost all sense of what it is fighting *against* and what it is fighting *for* will never be able to persuade the rest of the population of its arguments and thus will never represent any kind of threat to the dominant system.

Another part of this ideological dislocation is the undermining of our belief that the world of which we dream could one day come about. The abstract (and thus physically "unreal") *possibility* of a future anarchist society – without domination, exploitation and alienation – is something that has always sustained us in our struggle. *Another world is possible*, we like to remind ourselves. Convincing rebels that this possibility *does not and cannot exist*, that their resistance is futile, is an obvious counter-revolutionary strategy. O'Brien tells Smith in *1984*: "If you have ever cherished any dreams of violent insurrection, you must abandon them. There is no way in which the Party can be overthrown. The rule of the Party is forever. Make that the starting point of your thoughts".[21]

A similar message is being delivered by the postmodernists and spreading as a self-destructive meme within what should be the anti-capitalist movement. This tells us that the system we oppose *does not even exist* as an external objective reality but that, in Newman's words, we should instead look to "our complicity in relations and practices of power that often dominate us".[22] The reality of our repression and exploitation by a solidly-existing ruling elite is not only questioned in this way, but turned into an accusation against would-be rebels. The convoluted reasoning, cited earlier, which leads Newman to conclude that "the universal human subject that is central to anarchism is itself a mechanism of domination"[23] is not one that inspires revolutionary engagement. What would be the point, if we are dominated primarily by our own mistaken belief that we are being dominated? In any case, for Newman, history is just "a series of haphazard accidents and contingencies, without origin or purpose" and "we have to assume that there is no essentialist outside to power — no firm ontological or epistemological ground for resistance, beyond the order of power".[24]

For postanarchists, there is no objective reality beyond the fixtures and fittings of the society we know today – no universal human spirit, no innate desire for freedom, no essential belonging to community, species or planet and, therefore, no possibility of ever rediscovering that belonging. As David Graeber and others have pointed out, there is little that ultimately separates this vision of the world from the dominant neoliberal ideology.[25] Both world-views preach a general acceptance of the *one and only reality of fragmented industrial-capitalist society* and locate freedom within the individual "choices" that can be made inside that "haphazard" world. All we have to do is to sit back and enjoy the ride into the industrial capitalist future that is the only possible future available to us, give up all hope of revolution, accept the defeatist *newthink* of the Party's post-philosophers, reject the idea of objective truth, understand that two and two makes five and learn to love Big Brother.

1. George Orwell, *1984* (New York: Signet, 1950) p. 80. The original UK title is *Nineteen Eighty-Four*.

2. Orwell, p. 249.

3. Orwell, p. 265.

4. Orwell, p. 81.

5. Orwell, p. 217.

6. Orwell, p. 278.

7. See José Ardillo, *Les illusions renouvelables* (Paris: L'Échappée, 2015).

8. Michael Löwy, *Rédemption et utopie: le judaïsme libertaire en Europe centrale* (Paris: Éditions du Sandre, 2009) p. 40.

9. Gustav Landauer, *Weak Statesmen, Weaker People!* in *Revolution and Other Writings: A Political Reader,* ed. and trans. by Gabriel Kuhn (Oakland: PM Press, 2010) p. 214.

10. Saul Newman, *The Politics of Postanarchism*, https://theanarchistlibrary.org/library/saul-newman-the-politics-of-postanarchism

11. Renaud Garcia, *Le désert de la critique: Déconstruction et politique* (Paris: L'Échappée, 2015).

12. Garcia, p. 117.

13. Ibid.

14. Newman.

15. Ibid.

16. Orwell, p. 310.

17. Orwell, p. 212.

18. Orwell, pp. 50-51.

19. Orwell, pp. 52-3.

20. Orwell, p. 215.

21. Orwell, pp. 261-62.

22. Newman.

23. Ibid.

24. Ibid.

25. David Graeber, *Toward an Anthropological Theory of Value: The False Coin of our Own Dreams* (New York: Palgrave, 2001).

3

WHEN NEGATIVE IS POSITIVE

There has always been a destructive aspect to anarchism, whether it takes the form of broken windows or uncompromising calls for the shattering of the social status quo. This destructivity is only part of the story, but at the same time it is an *important* part and needs to be embraced rather than avoided. And it is crucial to understand that it arises from an overwhelmingly *positive* mindset.

The will to destruction is obviously targeted at an existing order which anarchists find entirely unacceptable. The defeat of this old order will pave the way for a new and better world – and this is, in itself, a fundamentally positive vision. But it goes deeper than that. Anarchists classically regard their better world as something that *already exists* on an abstract plane, as a *possibility waiting to be made reality*. There is a certainty that the society to which they aspire is not the "cloud-cuckoo land" derided by right-wing opponents, but something that *would really work*. Furthermore, it is not something that could, or would need to be, imposed by a "people's state", but represents the way in which the bulk of humankind would *wish to live* if they were freed (physically and psychologically) to make a choice. Explains the anarcho-syndicalist Rudolf Rocker: "For the Anarchist, freedom is not an abstract philosophical concept, but the vital concrete possibility for every human being to bring to full development all the powers, capacities and talents with which nature has endowed him, and turn them to social account. The less this natural development of man is influenced by ecclesiastical or political guardianship, the more efficient and harmonious will human personality become, the more it will become the measure of the intellectual culture of the society in which it has grown".[1]

The idea of doing away with all laws and authority does not make any sense if you believe that human beings are naturally brutal, selfish and greedy – or, indeed, if you maintain that the right kind of thinking and behaviour has to be drummed into them by a (state) system of education. It only makes sense if you believe that human beings have some kind of inherent capacity to live freely as what Rocker terms a "social organism",[2] in an anarchic condition of non-hierarchical co-operation and mutual aid.

This is certainly the theory behind Peter Kropotkin's anarchist response to the right-wing Darwinists' bleak view of human nature. He insists: "Nature has thus to be recognised as the *first ethical teacher of man.* The social instinct, innate in men as well as in all the social animals, – this is the origin of all ethical conceptions and all the subsequent development of morality".[3] It also remains an underlying assumption behind anarchist thinking at every level, even if this is sometimes implied rather than fully spelled out. For instance, in his book *The Philosophy of Punk,* Craig O'Hara complains of contemporary society: "Human beings act as if they have nothing in common with each other. It is as if we have all been brought here to function for ourselves in a way that does not include others".[4] Behind this negative lies an obvious positive, which could be translated as: "Human beings have much in common with each other. We are here to function for the collective good in a way that includes others".

If you believe that this *natural* potential for mutual aid is being thwarted by the structures of contemporary society, that "dictatorship is the negation of organic development, of natural building from below upwards"[5] as Rocker puts it, then it is not a "negative" thing to want to smash that dictatorial society to pieces. And there isn't even any risk involved, since you know that people will *naturally* re-form themselves into communal structures, rather than fall apart into the murderous "chaos" which right-wingers always identify with the absence of authority.

This empowering underlying truth declared by anarchists – that human beings do not need authority to "make" them behave well – has long been recognised as a threat by the dominant system and therefore furiously countered. The repressive implications of the prevailing anti-anarchist theory are clearly spelled out by Noam Chomsky when he warns: "If in fact man is an indefinitely malleable, completely plastic being, with no innate structures of mind and no intrinsic needs of a cultural or social character, then he is a fit subject for the 'shaping of behavior' by the state authority, the corporate manager, the technocrat, or the central committee".[6] This view is echoed by anthropologist Robin Fox: "If there is no human nature, any social system is as good as any other, since there is no base line of human needs by which to judge them. If, indeed, everything is learned, then surely men can be taught to live in any kind of society. Man is at the mercy of all the tyrants – be they fascists or liberals – who think they know what is best for him".[7]

Chomsky speculates that there is a connection between the ongoing dominance of the "empty organism" theory, despite its being "demonstrably false", and the ideologically-driven need to counter the anarchist belief that human communities can work (and indeed work best) without external authority. He writes: "One speculation derives from the question: who benefits? We have already seen a plausible answer: the beneficiaries are those whose calling is to manage and control, who face no serious moral barrier to their pursuits if empty organism doctrines are correct".[8]

Kropotkin and Chomsky both see an innate and invisible structure within human minds and communities, but neither of them is suggesting any kind of rigid or limiting version of human nature. Kropotkin sees evolution as a process of constant dynamic social interaction with the environment[9] and Chomsky's thinking, in his linguistic work as well, is centred on the idea of capacity rather than specific content. A human being is born with an ability to learn a language – *any* language – which will be activated by interaction with a specific language and will thus take on a definite content, he explains. As Robin Robertson puts it: "Chomsky's work points to a deep underlying structure that eventually shows itself as language".[10]

There are definite similarities between this concept of an underlying structure – so central to the anarchist idea of naturally self-organising human communities – and the theories of Carl Jung. Jung insists, in a direct rebuttal of the "empty organism" fallacy: "Mind is not born as a *tabula rasa*. Like the body, it has its pre-established individual definiteness; namely, forms of behaviour. They become manifest in the ever-recurring patterns of psychic functioning. As the weaver bird will build its nest infallibly in its accustomed form, so man despite his freedom and superficial changeability will function psychologically according to his original patterns – up to a certain point".[11]

Behind the invisible structure of our innate mind, Jung sees the existence of archetypes, which James Hillman describes as "the most fundamental patterns of human existence".[12] Jung himself makes it clear that these archetypes are very real: "Archetypes are not whimsical inventions, but autonomous elements of the unconscious psyche which were there before any invention was thought of. They represent the unalterable structure of a psychic world whose 'reality' is attested by the determining effects it has upon the conscious mind".[13] But, at the same time, like Chomsky's ability to learn language, they emerge initially in the shape of a capacity, a potential which needs to be triggered by contact with the outside world. Explains Jung: "They are eternally inherited forms and ideas which have at first no specific content. Their specific content only appears in the course of the individual's life, when personal experience is taken up in precisely these forms".[14]

Robertson makes the connection between Jung's theory of inherent content-less archetypes and "physicist David Bohm's hypothesis that there is an *implicate order* from which the *explicit order* of the physical world we know emerges".[15] Bohm himself, explaining Einstein's unified field theory, says: "Nowhere is there a break or a division. Thus, the classical idea of the separability of the world into distinct but interacting parts is no longer valid or relevant. Rather, we have to regard the universe as *an undivided and unbroken whole*".[16] Describing what he terms a "new notion of order", he continues: "This order is not to be understood solely in terms of a regular arrangement of *objects* (e.g., in rows) or as a regular arrangement of *events* (e.g., in a series). Rather a *total order* is contained, in some *implicit* sense, in each region of time and space".[17]

This is anarchist order, on a universal scale – an underlying natural capacity to take on a coherent structure. The basis for this coherence is always oneness. Individual human beings have an innate capacity to behave in socially co-operative ways because they naturally form part of a greater whole – a community, a species, a planetary organism. Elements of the universe together possess a certain kind of order, because they are all part of one cosmic whole. Different parts of one single entity cannot permanently disintegrate into multiplicity and chaos because they will essentially *always be* that one single entity, which has divided itself into a multiplicity of elements.

Writes Fritjof Capra, in his account of quantum theory: "It shows that we cannot decompose the world into independently existing smallest units. As we penetrate into matter, nature does not show us any isolated 'basic building blocks', but rather appears as a complicated web of relations between the various parts of the whole".[18] When discussion turns to quantum theory, the mind tends to conjure up images of outer space, distant galaxies and black holes. But the real relevance of this cosmic unity lies much closer to home. "Because the universe is an immense organic being, all the parts of the world are subject to the same laws",[19] writes Johannes Fabricius in a book on alchemy, and the physicists' discovery of overall order in the universe in fact confirms the age-old Hermetic wisdom of a single structural reality which manifests on every possible level. This is the theory behind the microcosm and the macrocosm, the *law of correspondence* which links inner and outer, lower and higher in one "unified field". It also fits in perfectly with the theories of Jung, Chomsky and Kropotkin regarding an invisible and innate structure within the human mind, ready and waiting to be stimulated by contact with the outside environment into taking on a more concrete content-bearing form.

But what happens when the inherent structures of the human mind, waiting to be stimulated by the corresponding structures of collective human society, find themselves confronted with the society we know today? Pierre-Joseph Proudhon writes that each human being "carries in his heart the principle of a morality superior to himself. This principle does not come to him from outside; it is secreted within him, it is immanent... Justice, in other words, exists in us like love, like notions of beauty, of utility, of truth, like all our powers and faculties".[20] When a human being, equipped with an innate sense of justice, encounters the rank injustice of the modern capitalist world, their natural response can only be one of disgust. This is a common reaction to contemporary society and individuals can cope with this in a variety of ways. Some simply push their feelings to one side and adapt to the world in which they find themselves living. The everyday details of their complicated modern lives and external pressures to conform "are so strong that they drown the quiet voice of nature", [21] as Jung observes. This is not necessarily the end of the matter, because the suppression of a natural reaction by what Herbert Silberer calls "another will, something determined by our culture",[22] will often lead to deep anxiety, hence the spiralling use of anti-depressant drugs, and other numbing addictions, in the industrial world.

Other individuals, who unfortunately are currently in the minority, refuse to suppress their natural revulsion at the injustices of society. Instead, in the words of the anarchist psychoanalyst Otto Gross, they are infused with "the revolutionary instinct of humankind" which "refuses to adapt to that which is inferior, to power, to subjection, to property, to habit, to tradition, to morality".[23] Note that there is a two-fold action involved in this process – the revolutionary is calling on both the particular inner strength of their own individuality and, at the same time, the universal human revolutionary instinct. Ultimately, these cannot be separated – the revolutionary instinct of the species *depends* on the strength of certain individuals to express it. It is only *through* the individual that it becomes physically *active*. This is why anarchists, in theory and in practice, always insist as much on the freedom of the individual as on the social welfare of the community.

Punk activist Mark Andersen urges us:

"Think for yourself, be yourself, don't just take what society gives you, create your own rules, live your own life".[24] O'Hara stresses: "It is not enough for a person to look different from the mainstream, there is an important emphasis on consciously becoming one's own self",[25] going on to describe a self-questioning process "aimed at making a person aware of himself and his own identity".[26] It is telling that he writes of "becoming one's own self" and being "aware" of one's self – implying, as one would expect from the anarchist tradition, that there is, indeed, a *pre-existing self* in there to discover, rather than the malleable empty organism proposed by the dominant capitalist discourse. "Punk is gut rebellion",[27] says O'Hara – according to my dictionary, this means it is characterised by what is "basic, essential or natural". This is the same gut rebellion as that voiced by Michael Bakunin when he calls for a liberty consisting of the full development of all the material, intellectual and moral powers that are latent in each person, "liberty that recognizes no restrictions other than those determined by the laws of our own individual nature, which cannot properly be regarded as restrictions since these laws are not imposed by any outside legislator beside or above us, but are immanent and inherent, forming the very basis of our material, intellectual and moral being".[28]

The rejection of society's laws, in favour of one's own inner laws, tends to lead to confrontation with that society and Gross regards this as being inevitable for any individual with the mental strength to stand firm for their own inner principles. He writes: "It appears that the real nature of these conflicts always leads back, in the last resort, to a general principle: the conflict between that which is proper to the individual and that which is alien to them, that which is individually innate and that which is suggested, learned, imposed from the outside. This conflict between individuality and an external authority which reaches into its interiority, tragically affects childhood more than any other period in life. It affects it all the more tragically if the personality involved is rich and powerfully original in its aptitudes. The earlier and more intensely that the capacity to resist authority and external intervention begins to take up its protective function, the more the wrench of conflict is aggravated and rapidly deepens and intensifies".[29]

This permanent state of conflict, caricatured in the persona of an anarchist rioter or an angry punk, might appear on the surface to be purely "negative". But, as should now be clear, that is far from being the case. The conflict is a positive revolt, the expression of an innate sense of justice, *the reassertion of natural order against the corruption of the modern capitalist world.* As Silberer says: "Whoever has his conscience once rightly awakened, has in his heart an endlessly burning flame that eats up everything that is contrary to his nature".[30] Hatred for contemporary society and rebellion against it are born of an unconscious awareness that this is *not how things are supposed to be.* We are born into the world with implicit expectations as to what we might find there, implicit needs from an environment that is supposed to activate and stimulate all that is best in us, bring out our full human potential. Sadly, all we find is artifice, hypocrisy, greed, self-interest, injustice, tyranny, war and deceit. "Aversion and hate, the opposites of desire and love, are not independent affections but depend upon the latter",[31] writes Silberer, and it is our desire and love for a world of our imagination, always present in its possibility, that inspires the aversion and hate we feel for the real modern world in all its ugliness and inauthenticity.

Negativity would be to *adapt* to our surrounds, to *compromise*, to *surrender* to all that we know deep down to be *wrong.* Positivity is to be found in resistance, in struggle. Our first, inner, struggle is to fight the modern world as it exists in our heads, as it tries to block our true self from emerging, developing, becoming aware of itself. And our second, outward, struggle is to fight the modern world as it exists in our society, as it tries to block the natural structures of co-operative human community from reasserting themselves against its all-crushing dictatorship. And both of these struggles are based on the awareness of a positive: an implicit organic structure and order to life, denied by the dominant system. "Revolt passes judgement on an existing disorder; but an idea of order is *implied* in any verdict of disorder, and *explains* it", writes philosopher Joseph Vialatoux.[32] Ananda K. Coomaraswamy argues: "To reform what has been deformed means that we must take account of an original 'form'".[33]

When we look out of a window in the middle of winter, we can only regard the season as being bleak because we have in our minds the memory of springs and summers past – and the anticipation of those still to come. When we look out at the grim industrial capitalist system which suffocates us, we *know* it must be destroyed because we see in our minds another world which we *know* is possible. This other world is what Martin Buber describes as "the image of a perfect space"[34] – a utopia nourished by the past but in no way limited by it, a utopia that exists on an abstract rather than a physical level of reality but which is nevertheless solid enough to serve as the foundation both of our rejection of the modern industrial capitalist system and of our determination to build a better future in its ruins.

1. Rudolf Rocker, *Anarcho-Syndicalism* (London: Pluto Press, 1989), p. 31.
2. Rocker, p. 11.
3. Peter Kropotkin, *Ethics: Origin and Development* (Dorchester: Prism Press, n.d.) p. 45, cit. Peter Marshall, *Demanding the Impossible: A History of Anarchism* (London: Fontana Press, 1993), p. 320.
4. Craig O'Hara, *The Philosophy of Punk: More Than Noise!!* (Edinburgh and San Francisco: AK Press, 1995), p. 8.
5. Rocker, p. 75.
6. Noam Chomsky, *Chomsky on Anarchism*, ed. by Barry Pateman (Edinburgh, Oakland and West Virginia: AK Press, 2005), p. 114.
7. Robin Fox, *Encounter with Anthropology* (New Brunswick: Transaction, 1991), p. 17.
8. Chomsky, p. 174.
9. Renaud Garcia discusses a definition of anarchy in Kropotkin's work that "allows us, for instance, to see in every human society an organism which lives in a form most appropriately adapted to the environmental conditions, by means of increasingly active co-operation between its constituent parts". Renaud Garcia, *La nature de l'entraide: Pierre Kropotkine et les fondements biologiques de l'anarchisme* (Lyon: ENS Éditions, 2015), p. 63.
10. Robin Robertson, *Jungian Archetypes: Jung, Gödel, and the History of Archetypes* (York Beach,

Maine: Nicolas-Hays, 1995), p. 107.

11. C.G. Jung, *Psyche & Symbol: A Selection from the Writings of C.G. Jung*, ed. by Violet S. de Laszlo (New York: Anchor Books, 1958), p. xv-xvi.

12. James Hillman, *Archetypal Psychology: A Brief Account* (Dallas: Spring Publications, 1990), p. 3.

13. Jung, p. 108.

14. Jung, p. 293.

15. Robertson, p. 166.

16. David Bohm, *Wholeness and the Implicate Order* (Abingdon: Routledge, 2002) p. 158.

17. Bohm, p. 188.

18. Fritjof Capra, *The Tao of Physics: An Exploration of the Parallels Between Modern Physics and Eastern Mysticism* (London: Flamingo, 1992) p. 78.

19. Johannes Fabricius, *Alchemy: The Medieval Alchemists and their Royal Art* (London: Diamond Books, 1994) p. 26.

20. Pierre-Joseph Proudhon, *De la justice dans la révolution et dans l'église*, in *The Anarchist Reader*, ed. by George Woodcock *(Glasgow: Fontana, 1986)*, p. 20.

21. Jung, p. 20.

22. Herbert Silberer, *Hidden Symbolism of Alchemy and the Occult Arts*, trans. by Smith Ely Jelliffe (New York: Dover, 1971) p. 48.

23. Otto Gross, *Psychanalyse et Révolution: Essais*, trans. by Jeanne Étoré (Paris: Éditions du Sandre, 2011), p. 147.

24. *Mark Andersen, handout, 1985*, cit. O'Hara, p. 22.

25. O'Hara, p. 22.

26. O'Hara, p. 23.

27. O'Hara, p. 24.

28. Michael Bakunin, *La commune de Paris et la notion de l'État*, cit. Chomsky, p. 122.

29. Gross, pp. 96-97.

30. Silberer, p. 156.

31. Silberer, p. 348.

32. Joseph Vialatoux, *L'intention philosophique* (Paris: Presses Universtaires de France, 1959), p. 84.

33. Ananda K. Coomaraswamy, *What is Civilisation and Other Essays* (Ipswich: Golgonooza Press, 1989), p. 8.

34. Martin Buber, *Utopie et socialisme* (Paris: L'Échappée, 2016), p. 40.

4

ESSENCE AND EMPOWERMENT

Sensory deprivation is a technique used to disorientate human beings. Sometimes it is harnessed in a therapeutic way, to induce a state of relaxing meditation. But it is also deployed as a form of psychological torture. If we are confined alone and in the dark, perhaps even floating in a tank of water, the brain loses all sense of time, memory is affected, hallucinations are common and suggestibility tends to increase.[1] The undermining of the sense of self and reality thus makes us vulnerable to delusion and manipulation – we become ideal *victims*.

A general sense of disorientation is prevalent in modern society. We find it difficult to see any meaning in what we do, to relate to the world outside us. The events which mark our lives seem random and we mostly do all we can to avoid staring into the existential abyss of our ultimate individual death. This confusion does not reflect an inevitable absurdity of the human condition, but is instead the result of sensory deprivation on a cultural level. We are effectively blindfolded in two directions at once. When we look outwards, our understanding of the society in which we live, the history that brought us here, the possibilities that lie ahead, has been obscured by what Guy Debord famously termed the spectacle.[2] He described a fake reality which is presented to us as the genuine thing, the passive world of employment and consumption, a multi-layered illusion, an urban labyrinth of TV screens and advertising billboards that keeps us trapped inside its own self-referential irreality and tells us that there is no other life than the industrial slavery it offers us.

Things have certainly not got any better in this respect since Debord wrote *La société du spectacle* in 1967... And when we look inwards, towards our essence, our understanding has also been blocked. This was originally carried out in the name of religion. But, because it was really *always* about social domination, the taboo has now taken on a secular guise to suit the times and has become a philosophical tool of the modern spectacle, locking us into a state of mental disempowerment. As I will explain, the way we are taught to think about ourselves and our surroundings is keeping us in the dark, blinding us to the knowledge of *what we really are*. It also, of course, blinds us to any awareness that we are blind to the knowledge of what we really are! Indeed, the very suggestion that we *really are* anything at all, that we even have an *essence*, is considered unacceptable from a narrow contemporary perspective.

If we wish to discover our core reality we need to look within ourselves, beneath the surface of external circumstances and the outward-facing personality with which we greet the world, and deep into the inner self that underlies everything that we are and do. "Know Thyself" is a maxim which was inscribed at the Temple of Apollo at Delphi and which is likely to have been passed down to the Ancient Greeks from the wisdom of even earlier civilizations. It has been cited by writers from Plato to Jean-Jacques Rousseau, from Ralph Waldo Emerson to Samuel T. Coleridge and even made a cameo appearance in the 1999 film *The Matrix*.[3] It is also an important phrase in the interesting contemporary religion of Wicca, which is itself a deliberate re-merging of Neoplatonist and Stoic thought with the pantheistic pagan world-view from which Greek philosophy originally emerged. Wicca specialist Vivianne Crowley explains in her book *Wicca: The Old Religion in the New Millennium*: "Carved above the doors of Mystery temples were the words *Know Thyself*. This is also one of the aims of Wicca. The Pagan mystery religions were systems through which their initiates came to understand the true nature of reality and also their own inner nature: who and what we really are".[4]

Crowley suggests that the true centre of our being "lies not in the rational world of the conscious mind, but in the depths of our unconscious".[5] She explains that her interpretation of Wiccan philosophy is very much influenced by the thought of Carl Jung, who himself found much inspiration from the interrelated traditions of pagan, Hermetic and alchemical metaphysics. Thus when she writes about "the older and deeper levels of the psyche",[6] she is very much referring to the collective unconscious of humankind as imagined by Jung. The act of inner self-discovery is therefore a process of going beyond the limits of mere individuality to access a level of collective being. She writes: "The process of finding the Self is akin to digging the tunnel downwards to the cave deep underground where the jewel of the Self awaits us shining in the dark on the central altar. Until this tunnel is wide enough, the Self cannot come to the surface. The work of self-development is making that channel sufficiently wide for the Self to rise into the daylit world".[7]

This psychological journey predates Crowley's, and Jung's, description of it by many millennia. It is the mythological descent into the underworld, the world of individual death, and the discovery there of a psychological reality that was previously inaccessible to us. The German-Jewish anarchist Gustav Landauer – himself heavily influenced by the Neoplatonist and Hermetic tradition by way of Meister Eckhart, Friedrich Hölderlin and Wolfgang Goethe – recommends this descent to fellow anarchists, in the form of a metaphorical suicide, in his 1901 essay *Anarchic Thoughts on Anarchism*. He suggests that anarchists should kill themselves "in the mystical sense, in order to be reborn after having descended into the depths of their soul".[8] Landauer takes up the same theme again in *Through Separation to Community*, an article published the same year, declaring that we must "allow ourselves to sink to the depths of our being and to reach the inner core of our most hidden nature".[9] He makes it clear that this inward-directed journey is not a *flight* from the world but an attempt to achieve an authentic *reconnection* with it: "Since the world has disintegrated into pieces and has become alienated from itself, we have to flee into mystic seclusion in order to become one with it again".[10]

One of Landauer's biographers explains that the ultimate aim is to realise that we are part of "the universal organism, which in Landauer's *Weltanschauung* is recognized as reality".[11] This is plainly the same process as that described by Crowley when she states: "If we go into even deeper levels of consciousness, we lose all sense of our individuality and melt into the last reality which I shall call the *unitive reality*. Here things are not discrete and separate; all objects merge into one another and all are part of a greater whole that is the cosmos. This is what mystics call the *Way of the One...*"[12]

The similarity is no coincidence, of course — this idea of union with the universe is central to Neoplatonist metaphysics. Plato, much less of a mystic than those he later inspires, nevertheless writes in *Timaeus* that the universe is a "single living creature containing in itself all other living things mortal and immortal".[13] Some 500 years later, in the third century of our own era, Plotinus lays the foundations for Neoplatonist philosophy by declaring: "The universe is one living organism".[14] He adds: "Your personality does not come from outside into the universal scheme; you are part of it, you and your personal disposition".[15] He describes, in *The Enneads*, the same discovery of the universe-within as later described by both Landauer and Crowley: "In that you have entered into the All, no longer content with the part; you cease to think of yourself as under limit but, laying all such determination aside, you become an All... By the lessening of the alien in you, you increase. Cast it aside and there is the All within you".[16] Plotinus's deepening of Plato's metaphysics might well be due to non-European influences.

Born in Egypt, in north Africa, he enjoyed a lifelong friendship with an Arab doctor by the name of Zethos and is known to have had an interest in Persian culture. He was under no illusion that either he, Plato or Greek civilization could be credited with originating the metaphysics he set out, and his writing displayed instead a "general assumption that all his system is contained already in the most ancient knowledge of the world".[17] The same idea of a mystical unity with the cosmos is central to the esoteric Islamic tradition of Sufism. This was partly an inheritance from Plotinus and other Neoplatonists, but was also reinforced by Persian and Indian metaphysics, particularly at the influential School of Baghdad between around 800 and 900.[18] Again, it is our short-sighted fixation on our purely-individual subjectivity that is seen as the barrier to broader awareness. As the ninth century Sufi mystic al-Junayd puts it: "Know that you are your own veil which conceals yourself from you".[19]

When we have descended into the inner self-discovery of Landauer's metaphorical suicide, and grasped the reality of our essential belonging to the wholeness of the universe, the implications ripple back towards us through all the intermediate levels of our belonging. As these ripples reach closer to our own physical subjectivity, they relate in a more concrete way to our everyday lives and inform our thinking in a practical and "political" way. For example we can see clearly that our supra-individual identity must necessarily also apply, in a manner that is more *particular* and thus more restricted than that of the universal, to the planetary life-system of which we form part. This realisation of our belonging to nature – to life as a whole on our planet – is at the forefront of the metaphysical battle between industrial capitalism and its opponents. If people can be successfully persuaded that *nature does not exist*, or that humans are *not part of nature*, then they are less likely to stand in the way of the machineries that eat up the living planet and turn it into the dead vanity of financial wealth.

On a still more particular level, we also belong to the human species. This entity is very clearly biologically defined and thus can be identified as a *living organism in its own right*, although one which takes the dispersed physical form of millions of individuals, constantly dying off and being replaced by new cells. Below the significant level of humankind, our circles of collective identity become more blurred, overlapping and multi-faceted. Humanity is as diverse as the number of individuals that make it up and there are no entirely clear-cut categories of ethnicity, culture or association with which we can divide it into reliably identifiable permanent sub-organisms.

However, these sub-organisms can take shape, and can deliberately be created, even though they may be short-lived and fuzzy at the edges. The *feeling* of belonging, no matter how vague, remains an important element in human self-fulfilment. This is a central pillar of Landauer's anarchist philosophy. *Through Separation to Community*, written more than a century ago, explores themes that are ideologically very relevant today. In a key passage, he accepts that the medieval nominalists played an important role in challenging the opinion of the "realists" of the day (today termed "essentialists") that various abstract notions, some of which were only constructs of the human mind, were actual realities on a certain plane. But he describes with dismay how this attitude led, notably through Max Stirner, to the elevation of the metaphysically-separate individual into a new kind of modern god. Writes Landauer: "Our task is to prove that the concrete and isolated individual is as much a spook as God. We therefore have to restore the wisdom of the realists that also exists. The objections against them throughout the centuries were important, but now it is time to realize that there are no individuals, only affinities and communities. It is not true that collective names are only sums of singularities or individuals; rather, individuals are only manifestations and points of passage, the electrical sparks of something greater, something all-encompassing. (Whether the generic cut and dried names that we are using are adequate, is another question)".[20] Landauer emphasises: "The individual is a spark of the soul stream that we know as humanity, species or universe".[21]

It is crucial to grasp that this definition of the individual as merely an aspect of greater collective entities in no way *denies* individual freedom. It is, rather, a denial of the *limitations* placed on human freedom by our psychological separation from the world of which we form a part. The journey of self-discovery that leads us away from our individuality and into our collective reality, eventually leads us back round in a spiral to *individuality in a renewed form*. The result of a metaphorical suicide, a lifting of the veil of individual identity, is an enormous sense of empowerment. My being is no longer confined inside a single, flawed, limited, mortal individual but is set free to expand into the infinite and the eternal. My awareness of a belonging to everything around me also gives me a deep sense of *responsibility*, which combines with my sense of empowerment to dynamic effect. Says Landauer: "I recognize the universe and thereby give up my individuality; but only so as to feel myself as the universe into which I am absorbed".[22] Crowley writes that ancient mystery religions revealed to people "all they were and all they had the potential to be".[23] This is a telling phrase. The word "potential" stems from the Latin word for power, *potentia*. Being free to fulfil one's *potential* is to be *empowered*. The word "possible" shares the same origins. Self-empowerment and the release of one's inner potential open up *possibilities* that are otherwise closed to us by our own psychology, hidden from us by the veil of our limited purely-individual identity.

Throughout the long and sorry history of domination in human societies, psychological disempowerment has always played a significant repressive role alongside the brute physical violence by which authority is always imposed. Time and time again we are told to "know our place". We are only peasants and have no right to challenge our lords and masters. We are uncivilized savages and must bow to the improving rule of a superior culture. We are women and thus inferior and incapable of determining our own lives. We are employees and have to learn to do what we are told. We are the public and must trust in our leaders. We are miserable sinners, creations of an all-powerful and distant God, and must bow our heads in shame at our unworthiness. A *reversal* of this psychological disempowerment therefore presents serious problems for those who would rule over us – as their reactions have shown us on many historical occasions.[24] Crowley notes: "Christianity condemned all magic – spells, incantations, herbalism, divination, weather lore – the whole gamut of activities by which human beings sought to control their environment. The Christian attitude was that these activities were not the prerogative of the ordinary men and women, but the prerogative of the Church with its monopoly on the line to God".[25] It is not the "prerogative" of the disempowered to rediscover that power within. No such tendency can be tolerated by the authorities. All such heretics must be crushed. Crowley describes how the real motivation behind witch hunts became increasingly clear. Originally, witches had been accused of blighting crops, causing animals to die or miscarry and so on. "From the fifteenth century on, however, there were also political accusations. Witches were accused of undermining Church and state".[26]

The history of the Christian religion in repressing any "heretical" thought challenging its monopoly on power in Europe is well known, but a similar process also took place within Islamic culture. Describing ninth-century Mesopotamia, Dr Ali Hassan Abdel-Kader writes: "Baghdād at that time was the spiritual and cultural capital of the Islamic World, and in this setting the Sūfī School of Baghdād flourished and was truly representative as such. Its influence spread far and wide, to the western countries such as Syria, Egypt, Arabia and Africa, and to the east as far as Khurāsān. This school held in itself all the preceding and contemporary mystic thoughts belonging to and within the reach of the Moslem World".[27] However, the school began to come under attack from conservative elements within Islam. "The sūfis were said to be promoting superstition and pantheistic views",[28] he explains, and "every member of the school, including al-Junayd, was publicly accused of heresy".[29] The crucial dividing line between what was theologically "acceptable" or not was basically the question of whether the immanence of the mystical Oneness included the physical universe, and thus humankind, or whether it was transcendent to the point of being separate. Pantheists and heathens took the former view and "proper" Muslims the second view, according to the authorities.

Al-Junayd, the subject of Abdel-Kader's book, adopted a cautious approach and managed to walk a clever line by extending the idea of an immanent One as far as he could, while still preserving the obliged element of a transcendent deity. His was a similar approach to that of Marsilio Ficino, the Renaissance translator of

Plato and Plotinus, who carefully tailored Neoplatonist mysticism to make it acceptable to the Vatican and to thus avoid the wrath of the fifteenth century Inquisitors. But one of Al-Junayd's friends, Abū al-Husaym Ahmad ibn Muhammed an-Nūri, was prosecuted by the authorities and, although eventually acquitted, died shortly afterwards. Junayd is said to have commented later: "Since the death of Nūri, no one has spoken about the essential Truth".[30] And what was the essential Truth that could no longer be spoken? Simply that human beings are aspects of the universal Oneness. As such, they are not condemned to "know their place" and obey the rules set up by those who declare themselves to be representatives of a separate authoritarian God. "This complete indifference to the laws of religion and the established customs of society may lead the sūfi to a special kind of libertinism, as the history of sūfism has shown repeatedly",[31] notes Abdel-Kader.

One of the more outspoken Sufis at the time was Persian-born Abu'l Mughīth al-Husayn ibn Mansūr al-Hallāj, who insisted that union with the divine makes the mystic what Anton Kielce calls "a free and living representative of the Divinity".[32] Al-Hallāj's use of the formula "Ana'l Haqq" ("I am the Truth" or "I am God") did not go down well with the authorities and he was arrested and charged with heresy.[33] He protested in court: "I am not proclaiming my divinity, but it is what we mystics call the complete Unification with the Divine Will ('ayn al-jam'). God is the Writer and I am only an instrument".[34] But his accusers were not interested in the subtleties of his position and al-Hallāj was put to death in 922. The political significance of his persecution is recognised by Reynold A. Nicholson when he writes of al-Hallāj: "His crime was not that, as later sūfis put it, 'he divulged the mystery of the Divine Lordship', but that in obedience to an inward call he proclaimed and actively asserted a truth which involves religious, political and social anarchy".[35]

This metaphysical sourcing of anarchy is well expressed by Crowley: "In Wicca, we believe that each of us has free will. We cannot have other than free will because each of us in our innermost centre is Divine".[36] Likewise, for Landauer "the core of anarchy lies in the depths of human nature".[37] He insists: "We must realize that we do not just perceive the world, but that we *are* the world".[38] The taboo which has prevented everyone – from Sufis to witches – from expressing this simple truth still exists today. Words such as "essence" or "universal" or "nature" are considered intellectually unacceptable in many circles,[39] along with any world-view founded on our belonging to an organic supra-individual reality. The ostensible justification may now be philosophical rather than theological, *but the underlying reason remains social* – to keep us all safely "in our place" and free from any fanciful notions of wanting to participate in life rather than just observing it, of wanting to help create our collective future rather than simply accepting what is ladled out to us, of refusing all authority other than that which speaks from inside us.

If only we could smash our way through this odious taboo once and for all, we would discover waiting for us an inner collective potential that would entirely transform everything we think and know – our world would be turned joyfully upside-down. No longer would we be prisoners in a metaphysical sensory deprivation tank, aware of nothing but the absurdities of our individual limitations and mortality. No longer would we be confined in a supine state of isolation, disorientation, suggestibility, dependence, gullibility, fear and obedience. Instead we would be free to breathe a deep sense of connection and belonging, of meaning and authenticity, of courage and empowerment.

"Let us walk proudly and hold our heads high;
For the Sky is our Father and the Earth our Mother,
And we are the children of the Gods".[40]

1. https://en.wikipedia.org/wiki/Sensory_deprivation

2. Guy Debord, *La société du spectacle* (Paris: Gallimard, 1992).

3. https://en.wikipedia.org/wiki/Know_thyself

4. Vivianne Crowley, *Wicca: The Old Religion in the New Millennium* (London: Thorsons, 1996), pp. 2-3.

5. Crowley, p. 82.

6. Crowley, p. 86.

7. Crowley, p. 224.

8. Gustav Landauer, *Anarchic Thoughts on Anarchism* in *Revolution and Other Writings: A Political Reader,* ed. and trans. by Gabriel Kuhn (Oakland: PM Press, 2010), p. 88.

9. Landauer, *Through Separation to Community* in *Revolution,* p. 96.

10. Landauer, *Through Separation to Community* in *Revolution,* p. 105.

11. Charles B. Maurer, *Call to Revolution. The Mystical Anarchism of Gustav Landauer* (Detroit: Wayne State University Press, 1971), p. 73.

12. Crowley, p. 81.

13. Plato, *Timaeus and Critias,* trans. by Desmond Lee (London: Penguin, 1977), pp. 96-97.

14. Plotinus, *The Enneads,* trans. by Stephen MacKenna (London: Penguin, 1991), p. 143.

15. Plotinus, p. 158.

16. Plotinus, p. 467.

17. Stephen MacKenna, *Extracts From the Explanatory Matter in the First Edition,* in Plotinus, p. xxxv.

18. Majid Fakhry asserts that "the first phase in the development of Muslim philosophy was predominantly Neoplatonic" – Majid Fakhry, *Islamic*

Philosophy: A Beginner's Guide (Oxford: Oneworld Publications, 2009), p. 3. E.G. Browne comments: "It was certainly the Persian sūfis who went to the greatest lengths in developing the pantheistic aspect of sūfism..." E.G. Browne, *History of Persia, I*, pp. 427-28 cit. Dr Ali Hassan Abdel-Kader, *The Life, Personality and Writings of Al-Junayd: A Study of a Third/Ninth Century Mystic* (London: Luzac, 1976) pp. 22-23.

19. Abdel-Kader, p. 175.

20. Landauer, *Through Separation to Community* in *Revolution,* p. 101.

21. Landauer, *Through Separation to Community* in *Revolution,* p. 102.

22. Landauer, *Skepsis und Mystik: Versuche im Anschluss an Mauthners Sprachkritik* (Cologne: 2d ed, 1923), pp. 7-8, cit. Maurer, p. 68.

23. Crowley, p. 3.

24. See Paul Cudenec, *The Stifled Soul of Humankind* (Sussex, Winter Oak Press, 2014).

25. Crowley, p. 17.

26. Crowley, p. 20.

27, Abdel-Kader, p. 47.

28. Abdel-Kader, p. 39.

29. Abdel-Kader, p. 37.

30. Abdel-Kader, p 41.

31. Abdel-Kader, p. 88.

32. Anton Kielce, *Le Soufisme* (Paris: M.A. Éditions, 1984), p. 139.

33. Abdel-Kader, pp. 45-46.

34. Abdel-Kader, p. 46.

35. Reynold A. Nicholson, *The Legacy of Islam*, p. 218, cit, Abdel-Kader, p. 46.

36. Crowley, p. 70.

37. Landauer, *Anarchic thoughts on Anarchism* in *Revolution*, p. 87.

38. Landauer, *Through Separation to Community* in *Revolution*, p. 98.

39. See *2. Denying reality: from nominalism to newthink.*

40. From the Wiccans' *Esbat Invocation*, Crowley, p. 56.

5

NATURAPHOBIA AND THE INDUSTRIAL-CAPITALIST DEATH CULT

Humankind's belonging to the living flesh of our planet is an essential reality of our innermost nature. A profound sense of this belonging will therefore always surface, time and time again, in the hearts and minds of each new generation, whatever the obstacles placed in its way by the dominant anti-natural system under which we live. The barriers to this metaphysical understanding have varied over the course of the centuries. Sometimes the barrier has been the hierarchical theological dogma that sets "God" apart from "His creation" and "man" apart from "nature", over which "he" has been appointed ruler. This same dogma has also often denounced any feeling of spiritual connection to the earth and our fellow creatures as being some kind of sinister "devil-worship".[1] Sometimes the barrier has been the idea that there is no such thing as "nature" and that it is merely an illusion, a projection of our human subjectivity. Alternatively this barrier tells us that nature is in fact deeply unpleasant and is something to be overcome rather than respected. Either way, the result is a justification of the wholesale destruction and exploitation of a living world of which we are told we do *not* form a part. We are instructed to accept that our goal as humans is purely the advancement of the human species at the expense of all other life-forms.

Because the awareness of our real identity as part of nature keeps re-emerging in the human spirit, the attempts to block it can become quite convoluted. A good example comes in the form of a book published in the USA in 1990 and the UK in 1991, at a time when there was a general upsurge of interest in "green" thinking. Dorion Sagan's *Biospheres: Metamorphosis of Planet Earth*[2] is designed to appeal to those of an environmentalist persuasion. Its cover features an image of the earth, around which is draped a female figure, presumably meant to be the goddess Gaia. Inside, Sagan sets out what may appear at first glance to be an argument based on an understanding of the natural reality of humankind. In order to reinforce this impression, he cites indigenous North American and Buddhist wisdom, Carl Jung, Henry Thoreau and

Giordano Bruno and, throughout his text, he includes hooks that are clearly intended to appeal to ecologically-minded readers and persuade them that he is basically on their side.

Early on, for instance, he declares that "far from being an inert lump of matter, the Earth behaves as a giant organism".[3] He continues in the same vein, putting forward an analysis that would not be out of place elsewhere in these pages: "The presence of life anywhere in the universe is a signal that the whole of reality is, in a sense, alive. Although there is little scientific evidence to support this view of universal life, Aristotle and other Greek philosophers who laid the metaphysical foundations for Western science, held similar views. In addition, some thinkers at the forefront of quantum mechanics, such as physicist David Bohm, believe that the mechanical world view is no longer supportable and that the universe (physical reality from the level of quarks to galaxies) displays features of wholeness that make it far more like an *organism*, an integral entity, than any collection of essentially unrelated atoms or parts".[4] This tone even extends to a call for action: "The only way to avert polluting the oceanic, atmospheric, near space, electromagnetic, and other commons is for the members of human nations to realize and behave as integral parts of a single collective entity or organism. Even if we don't recognize our planetary interrelatedness, it remains true that our destinies are fused and that we will live or die together, integrated, perhaps, into the life cycle of a single giant being".[5]

Unfortunately, though, it quickly becomes apparent that all of this is merely window dressing, designed to trick the reader into thinking that Sagan's argument is based on environmental sensibility – an impression that could hardly be further from the truth. The biographical information describes Sagan as a "sleight-of-hand magician and writer", but the ideological sleight-of-hand he deploys here is clumsy and blatant. His basic line is that nature benefits, rather than suffers, from industrial capitalism. "Human technology reforms the planetary body, creating a new system for all species to use",[6] he claims at one point. "Technology may be dangerous, but adding technology to nature makes nature stronger and more stable than nature without technology".[7] He even has the audacity to pretend, with pseudo-scientific authority, that pollution is something to be welcomed. Sometimes this argument comes across as simply laughable, as when he writes: "It would be difficult to wax poetic about medical waste, chlorofluorocarbons, and carbon dioxide. Yet smog can enhance the colors of a sunset".[8] In other passages he makes a serious attempt at more or less proving that "toxic sludge is good for you", to reference the ironic title of John Stauber and Sheldon Rampton's 1995 exposé of the greenwashing PR industry. "In the long run, undoubtedly organisms will evolve means of digesting technological excess",[9] Sagan assures us. And the end result will apparently be resoundingly positive for nature: "Our technical civilization brings into circulation and combines many substances – such as pharmaceutical compounds, metals (for example, the platinum of weapons and the copper of pennies), rubberlike plastics, and other synthetics that were rarely or never used by other organisms. Garbage disposals, jet airplanes, and factory exhaust increase the rate of atomic migration at the Earth's surface... Physicists have even synthesised elements that never before existed at the surface of the Earth. With world-wide commerce and computer communication, the flow of atoms intensifies. With the appearance of *Homo sapiens, all* the chemical elements for the first time became involved in the process of life, the biologically aided circulation of elements at our planet's surface".[10]

It is surely no coincidence that Sagan refers many times to James Lovelock in the course of the book. As I have written elsewhere,[11] Lovelock uses the idea of a self-regulating Gaia to suggest that we should take no action against pollution, arguing that we should perhaps instead regard industrial waste, like cow dung, not as pollution but as a "valued gift". And Sagan approvingly quotes the celebrated former NASA scientist's extension of his Gaia concept to suggest that environmental concerns about the effects of industrialisation are baseless: in a 1986 paper, Lovelock asks: "Could it be that our very deep concern about the state of the world is a form of global hypochondria?"[12] Since then, the veteran Lovelock, a long-time supporter of the nuclear industry, has made it increasingly clear that his theory about Gaia is not *in any way* combined with a desire to defend life from the industrial capitalist system. A newspaper article about his 2014 book *A Rough Ride to the Future* reports: "The scientist and inventor James Lovelock claims we should stop trying to save the planet from global warming and instead retreat to climate controlled cities". And it quotes Lovelock as concluding: "We should give up vainglorious attempts to save the world".[13]

Sagan's approach is very much in the same vein. Like Lovelock, he merely uses the theory of a living planet as a "sleight-of-hand" means of justifying its destruction by the capitalist system. To this end, he comes up with the ridiculous notion that the earth is "actually on the verge of reproduction"[14] and that the horrors of pollution are nothing more alarming than the birth pains of new entities. These new entities will be the "biospheres" of the book's title, artificial pods that will set off into space and allow humanity to colonise the universe. He suggests: "Someday people may be in the position of the shrimp inside the ecosphere, the captives and crews of biospheric starships sheltered in spacecraft that double as synthetic Earths".[15]

Why would people want to live like shrimps in synthetic earths, rather than like human beings on a real earth? Perhaps because, like Sagan, they despise this planet and look forward to its complete destruction! "It is claimed that a truly advanced civilization would be no more attached to the planet of its origin than a newly hatched chick is to the eggshell from which it emerges",[16] he writes. And he enthuses: "Once Earth's biosphere reproduces into biospheres, the Earth itself – our planetary parent – could be crushed like a sunflower seed with no threat of violence to life as a whole".[17]

Sagan adopts the approach common to most cheerleaders of industrial capitalism in presenting the future he predicts as a *fait accompli* – "Biospheres themselves are destined to arrive; there is about them an air of evolutionary inevitability".[18] This has always been the script for "progress". It unfolds as a matter of course, like the passing of time. There is no way of stopping it and anyone who tries to do so is guilty of trying to "turn the clock back". The idea of industrial or technological "progress" has been gradually merged with the idea of any kind of improvement in human life. This assumption was unfortunately swallowed whole by most socialists and anarchists of the 19th century who felt culturally obliged to present their social utopias in the context of technological development.[19] This manipulation remains in place today, with any resistance to the "progress" of industrial capitalism often branded as a reactionary attack on the social "progress" with which it is wrongly bracketed.

There was an alarming illustration of this phenomenon in France in 2014 and 2015, following the publication of *La reproduction artificielle de l'humain* by Alexis Escudero.[20] The book is an anti-capitalist attack on the bio-technological engineering industry, which is busy building a Brave New World in which the rich can buy designer babies and ensure that their children are superior in every way to those of the exploited majority. Escudero reveals, for instance, that the Fertility Institute in Los Angeles produces 800 test tube babies a year, of which 700 have parents with no fertility problems – these wealthy Americans like to be able to pick the embryo with the "best" genetic characteristics, and also to choose the sex of their child.[21] This is a profitable business with all the usual trappings – the first Fertility Show in London in 2009 attracted 80 exhibiting companies, ranging from specialist clinics to sperm banks, and drew in 3,000 visitors.[22] A report issued in 2015 estimated that the US fertility market was worth between $3 and $4 billion a year,[23] while in the UK it has been estimated as being worth £600 million.[24]

However, Escudero sparked controversy by criticising the way that the left had failed to respond to the growth of this sinister eugenics business, which has its origins in Nazi Germany. He complained in his book: "Debate on the subject: nothing. Zilch. Nada. As if being on the left and supporting artificial reproduction of humans necessarily went hand in hand".[25] The problem was that Medically Assisted Procreation (MAP) in France was being vociferously opposed by religious right-wingers, who particularly objected to the idea of babies being produced for gay and lesbian couples. Escudero made it plain that this was not his motivation at all. He was countering the liberal-left slogan "MAP for everyone!" with the anti-industrial slogan "MAP for no-one!". It was the business he opposed, not the sexual orientation of its customers. He also stressed that he had nothing at all against the DIY insemination technique often used by lesbians and that this did not in any case come under the MAP label. Left-wingers who championed the MAP industry because they felt it was socially "progressive" were falling into a terrible trap, he warned. He drew attention to a slogan used by French gay rights group inter-LGBT which had declared: "There is no equality without MAP!". Commented Escudero: "For the cyber-liberal left there is no equality without recourse to biotechnology".[26] He warned that this fascination for technology was drawing left-wingers far away from the positions they claimed to defend and into *de facto* support for the industrial capitalist system. "This cyber-liberal left is misusing the fight for individual freedom as a vindication of market freedom. It is confusing political equality with the biological uniformisation of individuals. Its dream is of liberal eugenics, of abolishing the body and using artificial wombs. Its fantasy is of a posthumanity via the technological re-creation of the human species. Behind the mask of transgression and rebellion lies an enthusiastic identification with technocapitalism".[27]

This criticism of an influential and vociferous section of the left prompted a hostile response. On October 28, 2014, there was a picket of a talk that Escudero gave at le Monte-en-l'air bookshop in Paris, in which placards accused him of lesbophobia, homophobia and transphobia.[28] Then on Saturday November 22 a group of opponents mobilised against a workshop he was due to give at the Lyons anarchist bookfair. A leaflet claimed that Escudero was joining José Bové and Pierre Rahbi in an "environmentalist drift towards essentialism, in the name of the 'defence of the living'". It declared: "No to LGBTphobia! Yes to the extension of the right to MAP! No to essentialism and naturalism!"[29] An eye-witness account published afterwards by Annie Gouilleux describes how the "fascistic" pro-technology contingent blocked the entrance to the room hosting Escudero's workshop, insulting people who were trying to get in. In the end, the organisers felt they had no choice but to cancel the meeting. There is a profoundly worrying ideological phenomenon in evidence here, which is identified by Gouilleux in her account. She writes: "It's obvious that from the moment people consider that 'human' and 'nature' are either taboo words or that they don't exist, then the discussion will descend into absurdity. Or fisticuffs".[30]

In his book, Escudero describes how the aim of the new eugenics will inevitably develop from merely screening out hereditary defects towards making people more attractive, bigger, more athletic, more intelligent. They will, in short be "better than humans – who are imperfect by nature". Leaving behind the out-dated human model, these new products of industrial capitalism will be superhumans, "posthumans".[31] This vision of the future, born of a mindset which regards nature as reactionary and associates technology with emancipation, leads very easily into the worst excesses of industrial-capitalist fantasy, namely the transhumanist movement. This cult, which originated in the USA in the 1950s, basically envisages that humans will soon outgrow the restrictions of their natural bodies and, thanks to technological advances, evolve into semi-robotic beings. They will have artificial bodies, with replaceable parts, and their brains will eventually be uploaded into computers, giving them unimagined mental powers.

Not so long ago, this strange vision was regarded as little more than a sci-fi joke, but it has increasingly become the religion of the technological avant-garde and is supported by businesses such as Google. One of its key texts is *Cyborg Manifesto: Science, Technology, and Socialist-Feminism,* written in 1985 by Donna Haraway, an American neo-Marxist and postmodernist academic who has declared war on what she calls the "knee-jerk technophobia" of part of the feminist movement. A gushing profile in *Wired* magazine explains that her opposition to the "back-to-nature platitudes" of "so-called goddess feminism" is based on the insistence that "the realities of modern life happen to include a relationship between people and technology so intimate that it's no longer possible to tell where we end and machines begin".[32] In 1986, Massachusetts Institute of Technology nanotechnology scientist K. Eric Drexler brought out *Engines of Creation* and 1999 saw the publication of *The Age of Spiritual Machines* by transhumanist Ray Kurzweil, an American businessman who works closely with the US Army Science Board, has been honoured by three US presidents and has been proclaimed a "genius" by the Wall Street Journal.[33] Another important transhumanist work is *I, Cyborg* (2002) by Kevin Warwick of the University of Reading in the UK. Here he predicts: "Humans will be able to evolve by harnessing the super-intelligence and extra abilities offered by the machines of the future, by joining with them. All this points to the development of a new human species, known in the science-fiction world as 'cyborgs'. It doesn't mean that everyone has to become a cyborg. If you are happy with your state as a human then so be it, you can remain as you are. But be warned – just as we humans split from our chimpanzee cousins years ago, so cyborgs will split from humans. Those who remain as humans are likely to become a sub-species. They will, effectively, be the chimpanzees of the future".[34] So this is how Warwick and his colleagues see human beings as we are now – as "chimpanzees" destined to be trampled underfoot by the rise of the new race of cybernetic overlords.

Whether or not these unhinged transhumanist visions are ever likely to become reality is almost beside the point here. The immediate danger lies in what can only be described as their morbid aversion to nature – their *naturaphobia* – and the way this insidious ideological meme[35] is encouraging support for industrial capitalism, even among supposed anti-capitalists. Writes Escudero: "While pretending to support freedom and emancipation, post-feminists and transhumanists nurse a boundless hatred of nature; hatred of the innate, of that which is given to the human being at birth; of everything that isn't produced, manufactured, standardised, regulated, rationalised; hatred of everything that doesn't quite fit, that doesn't work, that falls ill, of everything that isn't efficient and productive 24/7; hatred of everything which gets away and can't be controlled".[36] This attitude comes across very clearly in an interview with sociologist and queer activist Marie-Hélène Bourcier conducted by Christelle Taraud for the book *Les Féminismes en questions: Eléments pour une cartographie.* She declares: "We have to reinvent and rebuild a feminist theory that sets itself apart from the subject of biologically-constructed 'woman'. Let's not regard 'woman' as the subject of feminism, let alone its horizon. For me, it's fundamentally important – and, for that matter, interesting – to do so by inventing or reappropriating figures which are abnormal, inhuman or posthuman. Haraway proposed the cyborg".[37] Bourcier explains that she is pushing this latter vision "so that women, and particularly feminists, stop being part of a technophobic tradition" and "to destroy the notion of nature".[38] She says we need to celebrate the "good news" that if there is no more nature then we are all "the babies of techno-culture".[39] Bourcier's undisguised transhumanist naturaphobia is only the tip of the iceberg of a certain brand of left-wing ultramodernist orthodoxy that has become so exaggerated that it was even apparently possible for a high-profile French anti-racist activist like Clémentine Autain to declare that "nature is fascist".[40]

Despite his reputation as some kind of environmental guru, Lovelock fuels this same naturaphobia every time he announces that pollution is not a problem or that we should give up trying to save the planet. He has also explicitly supported the transhumanist approach, saying in 2014: "Our species has a limited lifespan. If we can somehow merge with our electronic creations in a larger scale endosymbiosis, it may provide a better next step in the evolution of humanity and Gaia".[41] Sagan, with his daydream of the earth being "crushed like a sunflower seed" as human beings float off into space in little artificial pods, shares the same twisted philosophy, based on a contempt for *everything that we are*, for the planet of which we form part and upon which we depend. This is not just naturaphobia but *vitaphobia*, a fear and hatred of life itself – a *Thanatos*, death drive, projected from the self-hating mind of the individual out on to humanity as a whole, on to the planet. How else, in fact, could we describe industrial capitalism itself, other than as a death cult, ever-hungry for the sacrifice of millions upon millions of living beings in its machineries, its contaminations, its wars, its abattoirs, its cancerous civilization?

Because nature and life are both *real*, the naturaphobic and vitaphobic industrial death cult also necessarily hates *reality,* to the point that it develops post-philosophies which *deny the very existence of objective reality*. It derides and fears everything that is *authentic* and is obsessed by the *artificial.*[42] Its complete immersion in *falsity* means that it is blind to the fact that the path it would lead us along is a complete dead-end. For, on the most basic level, the industrialist vision of a technological posthuman future is entirely divorced from the physical *realities* of industrialism. Even if post-natural posthumans managed to upload their minds (or, rather, soulless copies of their brains) into a virtual realm of their own construction, the objective reality of the world they thought they were escaping would not somehow cease to exist. Pollution would worsen as the technological world expanded, animals would suffer from its consequences, the food chain would be imperilled, the very life-system of the earth would be at risk. Their technological bubble would still be dependent on an outside reality and infrastructure. There would still have to be mines to extract the minerals to build the computers, oil and gas wells to provide the energy, waste to be disposed of, pipelines and cables to be laid and repaired, flood defences to be built or strengthened as the climate span further into extremities, cooling systems to be installed for the huge banks of computer servers, bolts to be tightened, cogs to be lubricated, mould to be wiped off walls, and so on *ad nauseam*. Even if all the hard labour was done by machines and there were further machines to repair those machines, who would repair these? Who would be doing all the dirty work, wiping the metaphorical bottoms of the immortal posthuman narcissists plugged into their ego-massaging virtual existences? A race of "chimpanzee" slaves maybe, the left-over essentialist scum who had refused to jump on the naturaphobic bandwagon to oblivion? There is nothing very "progressive" about this vision of "progress" which is in fact, despite the "radical" or "left-wing" posturing of those promoting it, an industrial-capitalist mutation of fascism. Here is perhaps the ultimate truth that these naturaphobes cannot face – that their technological dream is nothing but a dangerous nightmare. It is dangerous because even if it never comes true, its ideological distortions serve to *undermine anti-capitalism* and promote enthusiastic participation in a supposedly "progressive" industrial system that is killing our planet.

I suspect that behind the outward-projected *Thanatos* of the post-humanists lies *thanatophobia*, a fear of their own personal death and a refusal to accept its natural and organic inevitability – hence the fantasies about machine-assisted immortality which lead them to embrace techno-capitalist ideology. As Theodore Roszak asked, as far back as 1972: "How many members of our own culture would not trade in their natural body tomorrow for a guaranteed deathproof counterfeit?"[43] In this desire, these artificialists are themselves victims of the same lack of understanding that they are helping to maintain and worsen by promoting a hatred of everything real and natural. The individualism that forms a central part of their dogma is itself an illusion, albeit sometimes a necessary one on a practical level.[44] All of us are merely temporary manifestations of much larger living entities, the most obvious of which is the human species. As such, in some ways we cannot really be said to "die" when our time is done. The living entity itself exists in the form of constantly regenerating cells, or individuals, which are naturally replaced as part of the ongoing process. Trees do not die when their leaves fall off. Species are not "dead" as long as they keep reproducing. Immortality comes from the continuation of the species, or planetary life, the birth of new generations. The end of our individual subjectivity does not imply the end of the objective reality of which we form part.

There is an essential collective nature to our existence that does not limit or oppress us, as the anti-essentialists imagine, but which in fact sets us free to experience a broader reality. This reality extends beyond the human species to nature as a whole, to all that is living, to all that makes up the universe. Behind the transhumanist loathing for life lurks an almost spiritual yearning for transcendence. But this yearning is tragically misdirected. It has lost sight of the fact that universal connection *already exists* and does not have to be *artificially created* by means of industrial technology. The connection is there waiting for us, in nature and the cosmos beyond, if we would only seek it out.

It is not by cutting ourselves off from our innate and organic essence that we will find individual fulfilment and true immortality, but by embracing it.

1. The figure of the Devil as imagined by Christians bears an uncanny resemblance to the Greek nature god Pan and other horned pagan gods such as Cernunnos and Herne.

2. Dorion Sagan, *Biospheres: Metamorphosis of Planet Earth* (London: Arkana, 1991).

3. Sagan, p. 3.

4. Sagan, p. 4.

5. Sagan, p. 8.

6. Sagan, p. 125.

7. Sagan, p. 145.

8. Sagan, p. 18.

9. Sagan, p. 108.

10. Sagan, p. 41.

11. Paul Cudenec, *Antibodies, Anarchangels and Other Essays* (Sussex: Winter Oak, 2013), p. 42

12. James Lovelock, *Geophysiology: A New Look at Earth Science*, in *Bulletin of the American Meteorological Society* (April 1986) 67 (4) pp. 392-97, cit. Sagan p. 144.

13. *The Daily Telegraph*, April 8, 2014.

14. Sagan, p. 4.

15. Sagan, p. 36.

16. Sagan, p. 159.

17. Sagan, pp. 16-17.

18. Sagan, p. 6.

19. See José Ardillo, *Les illusions renouvelables* (Paris: L'Échappée, 2015) and François Jarrige, *Gravelle, Zisly et les anarchistes naturiens contre la civilisation industrielle* (Neuvy-en-Champagne: Éditions le passager clandestin, *Les Précurseurs de la Décroissance* collection, 2016).

20. Alexis Escudero, *La reproduction artificielle de l'humain* (Grenoble: Le monde à l'envers, 2014).

21. Escudero, p. 62.

22. Escudero, pp. 69-70.

23. *Fertility Market Overview*, May 2015, www.harriswilliams.com.

24. Maxine Frith, *You're big business now, baby*, in *The Daily Telegraph*, October 19, 2014.

25. Escudero, p. 10.

26. Escudero, p. 174.

27. Escudero, p. 12.

28. https://paris-luttes.info/retour-sur-le-passage-d-alexis-1978

29. http://www.mondialisme.org/spip.php?article2208

30. Ibid.

31. Escudero, p. 118.

32. Hari Kunzru, *You Are Cyborg*, in *Wired*, February 1, 1997.

33. https://en.wikipedia.org/wiki/Ray_Kurzweil

34. Kevin Warwick, *I, Cyborg* (London: Century, 2002), p. 4.

35. Theodore Roszak writes of "the anti-organic fanaticism of western culture". He explains: "Organism is spontaneous self-regulation, the mystery of formed growth, the inarticulate wisdom of the instincts. Single vision cannot understand such a state of being, let alone trust it to look after itself".

The extension of naturaphobic anti-organism into the political realm, specifically in terms of a fear and hatred of the instinctive self-regulatory wisdom implied by authentic anarchism, is clearly conveyed here. Theodore Roszak, *Where the Wasteland Ends: Politics and Transcendence in Postindustrial Society* (New York: Doubleday, 1972), pp. 95-96.

36. Escudero, p. 186.

37. Marie-Hélène Bourcier in Christelle Taraud, *Les Féminismes en questions: Eléments pour une cartographie* (Paris: Éditions Amsterdam, 2005), p. 53.

38. Ibid.

39. Bourcier in Taraud, p. 54.

40. www.piecesetmaindoeuvre.com/IMG/pdf/Entretien _avec_La_De_croissance_inte_gral_-3.pdf

41. *The Daily Telegraph*, April 8, 2014.

42. Roszak notes that "the whole process of urban-industrialism upon our tastes is to convince us that artificiality is not only inevitable, but better – perhaps finally to shut the real and original out of our awareness entirely". Roszak, p. 23.

43. Roszak, p. 97.

44. See *7. Necessary subjectivity*.

6

THE EYE OF THE HEART

Imagine that you are being held captive in a prison camp and that, with some fellow detainees, you are trying to escape. In order to do this, you manage to dig a tunnel from the floor of a cell into the outside world. But when the big day comes, you find you have simply surfaced in the courtyard outside, so you hide your traces and try again. This time your tunnel is much longer, but again it is a failure. You have arrived beyond the courtyard but still within the prison grounds and in sight of the machine-gun-toting security guards. Months later, you have succeeded in digging a tunnel that is already much longer than your previous attempts and must surely be about to take you beyond the final boundary and into freedom. But then you have to stop. Your tunnelling has brought you up against a massive concrete wall, sunk deep into the ground precisely in order to stop escape attempts such as yours.

There are many different ways in which one

could use this scenario as a political analogy in order to illustrate the limits of certain approaches. One might, for instance, regard a faith in the possibilities of radical change through electoral participation as being a very short tunnel that leaves the would-be escapees firmly within the same prison compound. One might regard the slightly longer tunnel as being akin to an anti-capitalism which fails to take into account the fact that the whole infrastructure of industrial society is *inherently capitalist* and that in order to escape capitalism we will have to escape industrialism. And one might regard the final tunnel as being an attempt at political thinking that, for all its far-reaching radical intent, remains very much contained within the superficiality of modern industrial-capitalist thought and is therefore incapable of sourcing the metaphysical depth which is necessary to break free from its self-referential limitations.

I would like to take a closer look at the last two of these propositions, starting with my insistence that an authentic anti-capitalism must necessarily be anti-industrialist. "Factories, machines and bureaucracies are the real pillars of capitalist oppression", Miguel Amorós writes in his essay *Elementary Foundations of the Anti-Industrialist Critique*.[1] I absolutely agree with him, but his insight is by no means shared by all those who terms themselves enemies of the capitalist system. This is not a recent ideological phenomenon, either. In his illuminating 2015 study, José Ardillo writes that "19th century social thinkers and agitators nearly all positioned themselves within the movement for scientific and technological progress".[2] He notes with evident frustration how this attitude has continued into the 21st century and even corrupted environmental thinking with its emphasis on "green" technological fixes, such as so-called renewable energy sources, for industrial capitalism's many problems. "It's not alternatives to conventional energy sources that we need to find, but a way out of this whole world of energy consumption that they have led us into", Ardillo rightly insists.[3]

E.F. Schumacher also calls for a wider vision in his classic book *Small is Beautiful*, when he writes: "Fossil fuels are merely a part of the 'natural capital' which we steadfastly insist on treating as expendable, as if it were income, and by no means the most important part. If we squander our fossil fuels, we threaten civilization; but if we squander the capital represented by living nature around us, we threaten life itself".[4] First published in 1973, Schumacher's book inspired a whole new wave of thinking that challenged the assumptions behind capitalist economics and spread the alternative idea of *décroissance* or degrowth based on his observation that "infinite growth in a finite environment is an obvious impossibility".[5]

Unfortunately, this idea has remained distinct from the main thrust of anarchist and other left-wing thinking. Partly, perhaps, this is because some of those embracing degrowth are naïve in other respects, and are effectively committed to digging the shortest tunnel in our analogy, imagining that somehow the machineries of "democracy" and the state can be used to bring about fundamental change. But there is also fault to be found on the anarchist side. Although generally less dogmatic than Marxists in this respect, many anarchists are still stuck within the broader sphere of industrial-capitalist thought. They fail to challenge the greatest myth that capitalism has created to justify its own existence – the myth of "progress", of "development", of the need for permanent "economic growth". Ardillo puts some of the blame for this on Murray Bookchin, the late American social ecologist whose brand of municipal anarchism has recently been taken up by the Kurdish rebels of the PKK: "Bookchin believes that technological development must continue; in his view, the liberation of humankind depends on this. According to him, criticism of 'abundance', that's to say the political consideration of a possible self-limitation based on simple methods and human energy, is therefore consigned to the scrapheap of reactionary thinking. It's to be regretted that Bookchin's views on energy and industrial abundance have had, and continue to have, such an influence on the opinions of a large part of the anarchist movement".[6]

Industrialism *is* capitalism. It is capitalism in the shape of bricks and mortar, of steel and concrete, of tarmac and plutonium. Its sole purpose is to make money, to enrich the few at the expense of the many and of the planet. An inability to understand this – and still worse to imagine that this *radical* anti-capitalist insight is somehow *reactionary* – represents a serious impediment to the revolutionary potential of the anti-capitalist movement. It prevents the digging of any ideological tunnel that can lead us out of the nightmare of unending capitalist "development", of spiralling environmental destruction, of a planetary poisoning which can only end in disaster. Why would any anti-capitalist want their thinking to remain *within the philosophical prison built for us by the capitalist system*, with all its capitalist assumptions about the purpose of life, individually and collectively? It is only from the specific capitalist point of view, in which its own continuation and expansion is equated with human improvement, that a rejection of the industrial direction appears to be backward-thinking or reactionary. From a point of view outside of that thought-system, the industrial-capitalist belief in infinite "growth" is revealed for what it really is – sheer insanity. Anti-capitalist thinking must position itself defiantly outside the system it opposes, reject all ideological perspectives that are based within that system, find its *own* ways of describing and evaluating the past, present and future of human society. Herein lies the only possibility of real resistance to the capitalist system as a whole. As Ranchor Prime writes: "Tinkering with the present system is not going to be enough. If there is to be real hope of a sane life on this planet for the coming generations, we will have to find a new way of understanding our place in the world".[7]

This search for a new way of understanding does not have to start from square one – we would do well to look for guidance from the way humans lived before the industrial era enslaved them. This was very much the approach of Mahatma Gandhi (1869-1948) whose resistance to British imperialism in India went hand in hand with a deep opposition to the industrialism which it brought with it. He wrote in 1909: "Machinery has begun to desolate Europe. Ruination is now knocking at the English gates. Machinery is the chief symbol of modern civilization; it represents a great sin... Railways accentuate the evil nature of man. Bad men fulfil their designs with greater rapidity".[8] His vision for India, betrayed by his capitalist successors, was a return to the simple village life his land had known for thousands of years. And this, he saw, was the only sustainable long-term way forward for humankind as a whole. Gandhi said in a letter to fellow independence campaigner Jawaharlal Nehru in 1945: "I believe that if India, and through India the world, is to achieve real freedom, then sooner or later we shall have to go and live in the villages – in huts, not in palaces. Millions of people can never live in cities and palaces in comfort and peace".[9]

Behind Gandhi's imagining of a village-based future (which, of course, need not reproduce the social mores of any particular village-based past) is what Prime describes as "the Hindu ideal of a simple life of dependance upon nature's goodness".[10] Once we leave behind the quantitative mindset of modern capitalism and its crazed obsession with the never-ending multiplication of needs and consumption, we begin to come back into contact with what Schumacher calls "the traditional wisdom of mankind".[11] In India, as elsewhere, this wisdom understands that nature is not a "resource" to be exploited but a living entity of which we form a part. Sevak Sharan explains: "In our Indian perception, *manav* means a human being who perfectly respects nature and *danav* means one who misuses nature. It is not wise to go against nature. History has shown that any culture that is not respectful to nature does not last long: it brings about its own downfall. Vedic culture, on the other hand, has lasted for many thousands of years and is still visible even now. It is called *Sanatan Dharma*, which means the way of life that lasts forever, is self-perpetuating and regenerating".[12] This ancient wisdom, this cultural belief in a stable natural harmony outside the linear "development" of industrial "progress", remains a potent inspiration for opposition to the capitalist system. Indian environmentalist Vandana Shiva describes how she met many people during her years fighting the construction of dams "and I found that they were all inspired by the idea that the river is divine, a sacred mother, and that trying to appropriate her water is like annihilating the very source of your sustenance. In fact I've learned that there is not one environmental movement in India that is not informed by the ecological roots of Vedic culture".[13]

The loud-mouthed and whip-wielding ring-masters of *El Circo Capitalista* have always poured derision on traditional ways of thinking that get in the way of their ticket sales and profit-margins, denouncing them as being primitive, reactionary, obstructive to the best interests of humanity as defined by their very own philosopher-clowns. Thus, when the imperialist UK state introduced the Charter Act in 1813, "Lord Macaulay argued in Parliament that it would be necessary to introduce English education in India at all levels so as to create an elite that was Indian in body, but English in taste and thought. He believed that Indian literature – the Vedas, Upanishads, Gita, Ramayana and Mahabharata – was primitive and bore no comparison to the value of European literature".[14] Authentic human cultures, and the non-capitalist life philosophy that they invariably enshrine, have always been regarded as an obstacle by those who would steamroller over everything real and natural in pursuit of their own wealth and power, as I have described elsewhere.[15] It is not for nothing that the spectacle of modern capitalism has pitched its philosophical Big Top in the United States of America. Not only was the cultural identity of the indigenous North American peoples ruthlessly crushed by the genocidal European invaders, but those settlers were themselves cut off from the cultures of their home countries. The rich West African culture of the imported slaves, including the spiritual practice of voodoo, was also systematically attacked by the ruling elite. As Angela Davies notes, the slaveocracy "sought to extinguish the collective cultural memory of black people in order to confine them to an inferior social space".[16] That process was to be continued by a new black middle class whose attachment to the folly of modern capitalism necessitated a rejection of the wisdom of ancient culture, she explains.

Another attack on a manifestation of this same human wisdom, so unacceptable both to the power-hungry Christian religion and to the modern capitalist world which it helped to create, came with the twisted cruelty of the witch-hunts. It was not just individual women who were targeted, but, as Vivianne Crowley sets out, "the remnants of the *Old Religion* of Europe, the indigenous Paganism that Christianity had suppressed".[17] Traditional cultures, *old* ways of thinking, cannot be tolerated by the capitalist system because they fundamentally contradict the *modern* world-view it has built up and imposed on contemporary society, in which the *only* way forward can be the *capitalist* way.

A measure of capitalism's success in this respect can be seen in the way that, as we noted above, even those who imagine themselves "anti-capitalist" still accept the fundamental assumptions of capitalism and consider it beyond the pale to question the existence of the industrial world it has manufactured. Too many anti-capitalists and anarchists also accept another, related, assumption of the modern world – that any form of spirituality is utter nonsense. There is a close correlation between anti-industrial philosophy and a spiritual outlook – so close that it is often difficult to draw a clear line between them. Gandhi's anti-industrialism, for instance, was rooted in his Hindu beliefs. As Prime explains: "Even the planet Earth has a soul, and therefore Hindus treat the earth with love and respect, considering her as their mother who gives them life and without whom they would die".[18] He adds: "In the Vedic vision of the world, consciousness pervades the universe and all within it. A human being, an elephant, a cow, birds, ants, trees, mountains, rivers and the planet earth itself – all are conscious".[19]

Satish Kumar tells Prime that whereas Western Civilization considers *human* life to be sacred, Hindus have gone much further and applied this to *all* life: "Therefore all life forms, not just human beings, must be revered and respected. This is the reason for being vegetarian, which is ecological in the deepest sense. Animal life should not be taken for our own purposes, nor should it be artificially created, as it is in the West where millions of cattle, pigs and chicken are reared for slaughter in factory farms. There should be a natural pattern of birth and death in the forest, on the land, in the air and sea".[20] The problem in India, says Prime, is that this spiritual awareness of our belonging to nature has been deliberately destroyed by the industrial capitalism originally introduced by the British Empire. "For nearly two hundred years Indians have been estranged from their own culture by English education. They have been encouraged to think in Western ways and to value the things that the West values. Their own traditional values have been marginalized. In many cases they no longer know what those values were or why they were held because those things are no longer taught".[21]

Across the world, then, humankind has been *deliberately* cut off from the cultural and spiritual beliefs that once informed its thinking, because these acted as ideological bulwarks against industrial capitalism. It hardly seems outlandish, therefore, to suggest that opponents of industrial capitalism might do well to *revisit* those beliefs in search of inspiration. It is certainly the case that a narrowly political level of struggle will not suffice to combat the all-pervasive totality of the capitalist system, which has progressively built up ideological defences which extend further and further into our collective thinking, imposing limits which are now so deeply ingrained and widely accepted that they appear self-evident.[22] We need to go much deeper, much further, in our quest for the roots of meaningful resistance. As Schumacher says: "We are suffering from a metaphysical disease, and the cure must therefore be metaphysical".[23]

In searching for these ancient anti-capitalist beliefs we should not be restricted by the *specific form* that these might have taken in the past and the now-obsolete socially-conservative attitudes with which they might have become historically associated, such as mysogeny, homophobia or the caste system. It is, instead, the *inner content* of these traditions which we must seek and in this context any specific genuine path we take will end up leading us to the same spiritual centre. In *Small is Beautiful*, Schumacher imagines an alternative economic system based on Buddhism, but he insists: "The choice of Buddhism for this purpose is purely incidental; the teachings of Christianity, Islam or Judaism could have been used just as well as those of any other of the great Eastern traditions".[24] Schumacher follows the likes of Adolf Bastian, René Guénon and Ananda K. Coomaraswamy in identifying what Joseph Campbell describes as "the fundamental unity of the spiritual history of mankind".[25] The theory here is that beneath the level of specific cultures and practices (*Völkergedanken* in Bastian's terms), there are elementary ideas (*Elementargedanken*) that are universal to humanity.[26] At the core of this universal thinking is the idea of a natural state of harmony and order, explains Campbell: "The Egyptian term for this universal order was Ma'at; in India it is Dharma; and in China, Tao".[27] There is also emphasis, in Schumacher's words, on "the hollowness and fundamental unsatisfactoriness of a life devoted primarily to the pursuit of material ends, to the neglect of the spiritual"[28] or "the pretence that everything has a price or, in other words, that money is the highest of all values".[29] Instead there is the conviction that "Nature is sacred, all life is sacred, the whole earth is sacred" and that natural harmony, *Sanatan Dharma,* has been disrupted by modernity: "Western industrial life has become desacralized".[30]

In his exploration of the differences between sacred and desacralised ways of thinking, Mircea Eliade stresses the way that the creation of "sacred" places and "sacred" occasions opens up our experience of life beyond the mundane.[31] Connections are made between different levels of existence and the historical linear time within which we are normally trapped is interrupted by our immersion in a time-outside-of-time, a kind of eternity. A holistic universe is revealed to us by "sacred" thinking, a multi-dimensional reality whose macrocosms and microcosms interact and interrelate on every conceivable level.

This idea of "levels" is something which is particularly unacceptable to modern industrial thinking, not least because such an approach inevitably places its own supreme values – money, material possessions, production, quantity – at the very *lowest* level of human activity. Writes Schumacher: "While traditional wisdom has always presented the world as a three-dimensional structure, where it was not only meaningful but of essential importance to distinguish always and everywhere between 'higher' and 'lower' things and Levels of Being, the new thinking strove with determination, not to say fanaticism, to get rid of the *vertical dimension*. How could one obtain clear and precise ideas about such qualitative notions as 'higher' or 'lower'? Was it not the most urgent task of reason to put into their place quantitative measurements?"[32] The very terms "higher" and "lower" are considered unacceptable in certain left-wing intellectual circles today, as they are seen to in some way reflect a hierarchical social approach and therefore to be elitist. This is, of course, a serious misunderstanding – although any attempt to explain that it is so because the terms *do not belong to the socio-political level of reality* is doomed to failure since the argument cannot be made without reference to something (ie: a level) that is deemed not to exist by those subscribing to this approach!

The switch into a "higher" way of thinking could be seen as a kind of sudden departure from the one-dimensionality of everyday practical thinking, not dissimilar to the creative mould-breaking "lateral thinking" promoted by Edward de Bono. In some ways we might regard "higher" as indicating "more abstract" and, at the same time, "more significant", because it is dealing with general principles with a permanent universal application rather than specific instances on a provisional physical plane. The "higher" mode of thought is more distanced from the individual's daily life, being a sort of zooming-out from the issues that normally concern us. But paradoxically it is also closer to the core of the individual and is thus at the same time a zooming-in. Explaining the quasi-universal use of the terminology, Schumacher explains: "'Higher' always means and implies 'more inner', 'more interior', 'deeper', 'more intimate'; while 'lower' means and implies 'more outer', 'more external', 'shallower', 'less intimate'. This synonymity can be found in many languages, perhaps in all of them".[33]

The fruits of this "higher" thinking are not the pragmatic considerations of the "lower" thought-processes, but something much more exciting – ideas! Writes Schumacher: *Ideas* produce insight and understanding and the world of ideas lies within us. The truth of ideas cannot be seen by the senses but only by that special instrument sometimes referred to as 'the eye of the heart' which, in a mysterious way, has the power of recognising truth when confronted with it".[34] He argues: "Only through the 'heart' can contact be made with the higher grades of significance and Levels of Being. For anyone wedded to the materialistic scientism of the modern age it will be impossible to understand what this means... He insists that truth can be discovered only by means of the brain, which is situated in the head and not the heart. All of this means that 'understanding with one's heart' is to him a meaningless collection of words... For him, in other words, higher levels of reality simply do not exist, *because his faith excludes the possibility of their existence*".[35]

The concept of the "heart" as a neglected organ-of-thought is related to the notion of an unconscious mind, both individual and collective, whose existence and significance has been stifled throughout the centuries by the life-denying dogmas of both organised religion and modern industrial society. "Christianity can be seen as the triumph of the conscious mind over the realm of Nature," writes Crowley from her pagan perspective, for instance. "The Gods were no longer to be seen as within Nature, but outside it. Nature was no longer sacred and holy, but the creation of a transcendent father (without the mother). Our conscious minds learned to suppress the unconscious and keep it at bay".[36] For the alchemist tradition, says Johannes

Fabricius, the search for treasures hidden deep inside the Earth is "a symbol for their penetration of the 'crust' of consciousness and for their discovery of the treasure hidden beneath it in the darkness of the unconscious".[37] Martin Lings explains that this same idea is also significant in Islamic thought and that "the Quranic perspective agrees with that of the whole ancient world, both of East and of West, in attributing vision to the heart and in using this word to indicate not only the bodily organ of that name but also what this corporeal centre gives access to, namely the centre of the soul, which itself is the gateway to a higher 'heart', namely the Spirit".[38]

The heart, or the unconscious, is the organ of our human spirituality, whose "higher" taste and perspective allows us to look down with disdain on the plastic-wrapped fast-food meal of appearance, money and possessions served up to us at the uninspiring philosophical banquet of industrial-capitalist thought. This spirituality will never be destroyed. It is a quality that survives deep within us and is reborn with each new generation. However, for those who have to grow up in the deadness of the modern world, whose so-called "religions" are mostly nothing more than controlling constructs of the dominant socio-economic system,[39] it is difficult to find a framework in which to express this inherent spirituality. We search for *meaning*, search for *magical* experiences, search for a deeper and more vibrant sense of *being*. But, thanks to the narrow and spirit-denying orthodoxies of the ideological thought police who patrol the boundaries of permissible opinion, this yearning is kept apart from any political engagement. We are forbidden from making the crucial connection between our thwarted desire to *really live* and the need to shake off the physical and mental shackles of industrial capitalism. We are warned off listening to our *hearts* – "the faculty of direct spiritual (or intellectual) vision"[40] – and are thus steered away from unleashing the metaphysical uprising that could set human beings free to be everything they have the potential to be.

This uprising, this *"metanoia"*[41] or "Great Turning",[42] will take place on the vibrant "higher" level of being whose existence is denied by the defenders of monochromatic industrial flatness: a level of being on which we are not merely isolated individual units, but vital manifestations of organic collective nature and flashing glints in the eye of the eternal cosmos. This does not mean that it will not *also* take place on the everyday social level – and the depth of the anarchist vision makes it particularly capable of bridging these levels, I have argued elsewhere[43] – but it cannot succeed if it *only* unfolds on what is regarded as the "political" plane. We must rediscover our belonging to the living universe of which we will always be part, rediscover the ancient wisdom which told of us of this belonging, understand the ways in which this belonging has been hidden from us by an industrial death-dogma which has even contaminated ideologies which seem to preach resistance. That way, when our metaphysical tunnel reaches the final perimeter wall of the industrial capitalist prison, we will have dug deep enough to pass underneath its confining ideological concrete and finally escape to the glorious freedom of *Sanatan Dharma,* the natural harmony that is the ultimate aim of genuine anarchism.

1. Miguel Amorós, *Fondements élémentaires de la critique anti-industrielle*, in *Préliminaires: Une perspective anti-industrielle* (Villsavary: Éditions de la Roue, 2015), p. 60.

2. José Ardillo, *Les illusions renouvelables* (Paris: L'Échappée, 2015), p. 91.

3. Ardillo, p. 229.

4. E.F. Schumacher, *Small is Beautiful: A Study of Economics As If People Mattered* (London: Abacus, 1974), p. 13.

5. Schumacher, *Small is Beautiful,* p. 40.

6. Ardillo, pp. 127-28.

7. Ranchor Prime, *Vedic Ecology: Practical Wisdom for Surviving the 21st Century* (Novato, California:

Mandala, 2002), p. 154.

8. Mahatma Gandhi, *Hind Swaraj*, 1909, cit. Prime, p. 86.

9. Gandhi, letter to Nehru, October 5, 1945, cit. Prime p. 91.

10. Prime, p. 65.

11. Schumacher, *Small is Beautiful*, p. 250.

12. Prime, p. 36.

13. Prime, pp. 130-31.

14. Prime, p. 101.

15. Paul Cudenec, *The Stifled Soul of Humankind* (Sussex: Winter Oak, 2014).

16. Angela Y. Davies, *Blues Legacies and Black Feminism* (New York: Random House, 1998) p. 155.

17. Vivianne Crowley, *Wicca: The Old Religion in the New Millennium* (London: Thorsons, 1996), p. 30.

18. Prime, p. 43.

19. Prime, p. 47.

20. Prime, p. 96.

21. Prime, pp. 148-49.

22. See *2. Denying reality: from nominalism to newthink*.

23. Schumacher, *Small is Beautiful*, p. 83.

24. Schumacher, *Small is Beautiful*, p. 43.

25. Joseph Campbell, *The Masks of God: Primitive Mythology* (London: Souvenir Press, 2011), p. 5.

26. Campbell, p. 32.

27. Campbell, p. 149.

28. Schumacher, *Small is Beautiful*, p. 31.

29. Schumacher, *Small is Beautiful*, p. 38.

30. Prime, p. 103.

31. Mircea Eliade, *Le sacré et le profane* (Paris: Gallimard, 1987).

32. E.F. Schumacher, *A Guide for the Perplexed* (London: Jonathan Cape, 1977), p. 20.

33. Schumacher, *A Guide for the Perplexed*, p. 43.

34. Schumacher, *A Guide for the Perplexed,* p. 58.

35. Schumacher, *A Guide for the Perplexed,* pp. 54-55.

36. Crowley, p. 181.

37. Johannes Fabricius, *Alchemy: The Medieval Alchemists and their Royal Art* (London: Diamond Books, 1994), p. 21.

38. Martin Lings, *What is Sufism?* (London: George Allen & Unwin, 1975), p. 48.

39. Witness the rise of Christianity as the official religion of the Roman Empire.

40. Lings, p. 51.

41. Schumacher, *A Guide for the Perplexed,* p. 153.

42. "The term 'The Great Turning', popularized by Joanna Macy and David Korten, describes the movement from an industrial-growth society to a life-sustaining one". Helen Moore, *Ecozoa* (Hampshire: Permanent Publications, 2015), p. 80.

43. Paul Cudenec, *The Anarchist Revelation* (Sussex: Winter Oak, 2013).

7

NECESSARY SUBJECTIVITY

The slogan "think globally, act locally", sometimes attributed to Raoul Vaneigem,[1] has become something of a cliché since it became common in the environmental movement in the 1970s. But it nicely reverses the advice handed out by a capitalist system which recommends we think only of ourselves and our immediate surroundings and, at the same time, step back with a sense of disempowered resignation from the apparent impossibility of ever "changing the world". And it provides us with a useful concept of transcending the limits of a false "either/or" choice in order to act simultaneously in two different modes. The phrase might usefully be expanded beyond the day-to-day level to guide us along the difficult existential path that we all have to tread. The "globally" could be extended outwards to the universal and the "locally" extended inwards to the individual vantage point, leaving us with "think objectively, act subjectively". And here I will be suggesting that it is just this combination we need to embrace so that we can be fully and actively human – *an awareness of the objective reality of the world around us and a necessary subjectivity which provides the means to help shape it.*

To this effect, I would like to begin by considering the standard definition of the word "universe". My dictionary says that it describes "all existing matter, energy and space". The fact that the universe is defined specifically in this way poses questions about what the dictionary writers mean by the term. No matter how inclusive that definition initially appears to be, it leaves open the potential for exclusion, for non-accepted material to be left outside of its imagined limits. And this rules out all-inclusivity. "A defined One would not be the One-Absolute",[2] as the philosopher Plotinus observes. We are left to wonder about the elements that lie outside their definition. Can an *idea*, for instance, be labelled as matter, energy or space? Perhaps if it is being *thought* by someone, it could arguably be regarded as a property of their physical mind, but the *idea itself* remains beyond physical definition. And how about clearly non-personal abstract concepts, like number? The existence of numbers (as opposed to the figures representing them, which are only human-constructed symbols) is real on an abstract level. The existence of the number 13 does not *depend* on the existence of 13 apples or 13 pencils. The fact that apples or pencils can be used to *illustrate* the number 13 indicates that the dependence is, in fact, the other way round. The abstract "13" is a pre-condition for the physical existence of 13 apples, pencils or anything else. Again, it could be argued that numbers *do* exist in the minds of actual people, and thus could be said to arise from physical existence. But that is not the *seat* of their existence. They do not need to actually be "thought" – let alone written down or represented by actual objects – in order to exist. If, somehow, every living being managed to banish the idea of the number 13 from their heads, would 12 items plus another one result in anything other than 13?

Numbers are neither matter, energy nor space but are still very much part of the make-up of the universe. Plotinus regarded them as constituting, along with ideas, something he termed "the Intellectual-Principle".[3] The same applies to other abstracts, such as capacities and possibilities. The capacity of things in the universe to possess spatial dimensions, for example, is undeniably real. If they did not have that capacity, they could not exist on the physical plane. Possibilities are also real. There must necessarily be the possibility of something happening in order for it to happen. As Ananda K. Coomaraswamy notes: "The impossible never happens; what happens is always the realisation of a possibility".[4] If there were no possibilities, there would be no existence, nothing would ever happen. And yet capacities and possibilities are excluded from the "official" definition of the universe.

If I were to throw a party, announce that "everyone" was invited, and then proceed to list all the kinds of people that this term included (friends, relatives, neighbours), I would raise the suspicion that I was, in fact, trying to exclude one or more persons who would slip through the net of my definition of "everyone". If I really meant "everyone", I would simply say "everyone" without qualification. In the same way, the term "universe" does not mean "all that there is" if it is limited in any way. By using the term "universe" but subtly excluding anything that does not fit into their idea of reality (namely "existing matter, energy and space"), those who share the worldview of the dictionary-writers are presenting a so-called "universe" that is not what it appears to be.

They are also leaving a gaping logic-hole in our potential understanding. If numbers do not actually exist *within* the universe, where *do* they exist? Likewise with the *capacity* to be or do something and the *possibility* of something happening. How can any part of the universe be said to have the capacity or possibility of doing anything at all, if capacities and possibilities are *not part of the universe*? Are these abstracts seen as existing in some realm of abstraction *outside* the defined limits of the universe? What are the implications of this? A universe that has to allow for the possibility of something beyond itself? A universe with borders?

If so, it is also a universe with disputed borders. The separation of "non-existent" principles, or abstracts, from the "existent" things they describe causes further logical difficulties. When abstracts such as number or possibility become physically real (such as when there are 13 apples rather than just the concept of "13") do they suddenly, then, spring into the universe without warning? Is their origin considered to come from beyond the universe? Or are they somehow seen as being *created* by the physical level on which they are represented? Does this back-to-front point of view suggest that the existence of 13 apples calls into being, retrospectively (as it were) and from out of nowhere, the possibility of "13"? There is a certain dishonesty here, which can be traced back to the use of the word "universe" – or, as far as my hypothetical party goes, the word "everyone". Both words, through their root meanings ("universe" means "all together") imply complete inclusivity but, as we have seen, this is not the case. Using the words as if they meant what they appear to mean, while knowing that the fullness of the term is limited, is an act of deception. By announcing that I am inviting "everyone" to my party and then subtly limiting the definition of "everyone" to potentially exclude someone who is not welcome, I am trying to appear to be something that I am not. In forcibly evicting abstracts from their physical-plane "universe", the dictionary-writers and their allies are simply restating their personal belief that these abstracts do not exist in themselves, that reality is limited to the purely physical ("matter, energy and space"). Their use and limited definition of the universe is therefore a *disguised ideological manoeuvre*, designed to exclude certain ways of seeing existence that do not meet with their approval, in the same way that my use and limited definition of the word "everyone" is an exclusion of certain people who do not meet with my approval, disguised as all-embracing generosity.

Needless to say, I am not here suggesting that the actual writers of the dictionary, or any other specific texts, are deliberately conspiring to impose this limited definition of "universe" upon us. Their attitude is merely part of the culture of the moment, the contemporary world-view which shapes and limits our thinking, and the potential for our thinking, on so many levels. It is part of the modern blindness. The "rational" view of the world expressed by the dictionary definition arises from what is now a rather old-fashioned "scientific" outlook. This outlook is the religion of the industrial era and has necessarily become dominant in our culture in order to internally justify the way our civilization functions. Part of any dogma is the self-defensive aspect that insists that this dogma is an unquestionable truth and here the modern industrial dogma is no exception. The movement of society away from the appreciation of abstract ideas or principles, and towards a limited, purely physical, definition of reality is presented as movement towards enlightenment. Contingent reality, the way things are right here and now under our noses, is presented as the only reality. The 13 apples are *real* and the number 13 is merely *descriptive* of that reality. There is no such thing as the essential reality of something. There are no universal principles beneath the surface of physical reality. Human beings are nothing more than flesh-and-blood machines, whose behaviour is "constructed" and can be "programmed" into them. There is no such thing as "spirit", because it cannot be scientifically identified or measured. The natural world is not a living being, but a resource to be exploited. The only possible world is the one we live in. Industrial civilization is the only destination at which humankind could ever have arrived. The continuation of that industrial civilization is the only possible future open to us. Anyone who says otherwise is a fool or charlatan. Nobody who challenges the fundaments of the dogma can be taken seriously. *Indeed, nobody who calls the dogma "a dogma" can be taken seriously, for there has never been a dogma which calls itself such, or could tolerate being identified as such.*

It is strange how blinded people can be to the existence of a dogmatic intellectual culture, when they themselves form part of it.[5] Suppose we lived in a society which believed, for instance, that before human beings are born, they enjoy a kind of pre-existence as bees. That whole culture would be built around honouring bees, making sure they were happy, examining the behaviour of bees for portents of future human lives to come, identifying individual bees who might soon become the hoped-for child of a human couple. Literature, art, poetry, music – all would be packed with references to bees in a way that to our eyes would seem insane. And yet, for members of that society, the bee-obsession would not only *not* seem insane, but would not even be seen to *exist*. "What bee *'obsession'*? That's just the way things are". Their language would, moreover, make it impossible to easily distinguish between bees as physical living insects and bees as the custodians of future human souls. To challenge the whole bee theory would not only be unthinkable heresy but also virtually impossible, as it would be taken as claiming that bees themselves did not exist.

In my writing, I have often tried to challenge the underlying dogma of contemporary industrial civilization – or at least to hurl a few pebbles of defiance in its general direction. I have discovered that it is very difficult to do so within the restrictions imposed by the language of that civilization, which means too much time and energy has to be spent on justifying or deconstructing the meanings of words. The way that the culture appropriates and redefines the symbols of our vocabulary to reflect its own ideological assumptions makes it difficult to pull clear of its gravitational field and express ideas which have no place within its dogma. This is very much the case with my intention here to go beyond the purely terrestrial sphere and discuss the universe. It is hard to do so by using an understanding of the universe that is confined to the physical plane and which, moreover, denies the existence of any other plane. I am therefore going to avoid the need to continually explain my own broader definition of the universe by using instead the term The Universe, with capital letters. And what do I mean by it? Simply "all there is", "all together", "everything". There is nothing outside The Universe. The Universe is itself the definition of all-inclusivity.[6]

Here are two statements about objective truth. *1. It is impossible for us to be completely objective about the truth. 2. There is such a thing as completely objective truth.* Why is it impossible for us to be completely objective? The problem is that, as scientists have demonstrated, it is impossible to be present in a system – even as a mere observer – and to be objective about what takes place within it. If The Universe is a system in which we are present, then we cannot be objective about anything that happens in The Universe. This is not difficult to grasp and needs no further explanation. But what about the second statement, that there *is* such a thing as objective truth? This is also easy to understand, but confusion sometimes arises when people mistakenly imagine that it is disproved by the first statement. This is not logically so. It does not follow that because we cannot ascertain the nature of an objective truth, then that objective truth does not exist. A goldfish in a bowl will never be able to look at the bowl, and at himself swimming around the bowl, and gain an objective impression of it. But the bowl, containing the goldfish, exists nonetheless.

Different historians describing the same episode will all present different, subjective, versions of the truth. No matter how hard they try to be completely objective, they cannot succeed. Two former lovers describing the break-up of their relationship will do so in different ways – maybe radically different, maybe just subtly so. That is inevitable, because each experienced what happened from their own subjective vantage point. Any "outside" account can only be dependent on various subjective versions, so objectivity is not possible there either. In both these cases it is perhaps unclear, at first glance, as to whether there is even an objective truth that *could* be described. Neither the nuances and complications of the social processes described by historians, nor the unspoken tensions and ever-twisting emotions that make up human relationships form obvious objective realities in the manner of a goldfish bowl. The objective truth behind what happens between people is something that could probably never be fully described with the limited tools of language, even if objectivity were magically made possible. But it is still there. Its existence does not *depend* on the ability of some theoretical outside agent to describe it in all its shifting detail and complexity.[7]

An actual sequence of events *did occur* in order to create the historical event or the relationship break-up. Actual objective truth *does exist*, even though it remains inaccessible to us. It is not truth that is subjective, just our experience of it. The ultimate objective truth is that there is such a thing as The Universe and that it embraces everything, without exception. This means, of course, that we are part of The Universe – not just present within it, but *part* of it. We are nothing else but The Universe. Our essence is entirely of The Universe. We are all twigs on the same tree, limbs on the same universal body. If we use modelling clay to make the figure of a little man, does the clay stop being clay when it forms a shape? Does it turn into "the figure of a little man"? If so, does it miraculously become mere clay again when the figure is rolled up and added back into the rest of the clay? Or is it always clay, but just taking on various temporary forms?[8] On the other hand, although our essence is of The Universe, our particular form is human and we have to adopt human subjectivity in order to live. The little clay man still *takes on* the shape of a man, even though he is *made* of clay. We have to inhabit our bodies. We have to eat, drink, defecate, exercise, wash and so on. We have to be ourselves *in order to be human beings*. We have to think inside our own heads, speak through our own mouths.

This is not a problem for us – that's what we do all the time without thinking about it. We live our human lives with a *necessary subjectivity* which is built into our bodies. We only see and hear what is around us (even if that consists of artificial images from elsewhere). We can only touch that which is within physical reach.

Imagine if we weren't limited in that way. Imagine, for example, that our universal essence allowed us to see through all the eyes of the human species at once. What a dream, to be able to see everything that every other human being could see, all the time, everywhere on the planet! And yet, of course, what a nightmare as well. My brain would be overwhelmed by the visual input of an entire species, billions of exotic faces and places streaming simultaneously into my head. How could I focus on chopping up a cabbage for my dinner? We are all limited by the physical form we take. That is what each of us is – a specific physical limitation of The Universe. And part of that necessary limitation is our subjectivity.

I have been using the words "essence" and "essential" and I am aware that this requires some explanation, if only because "essentialism" is sometimes deployed as a term of abuse. The kind of "essence" that people usually take exception to exists on a purely social or political level. It is, as I set out elsewhere in this book, a *fake* definition of essence which sets out to limit and constrain human potential within a certain pre-ordained social framework. I am not using the idea in this way at all and I am very wary of the use of the term "essence" in relation to any sub-categories within humanity. However, I would talk about essential *human* nature. The definition of a human being is clear and uncontroversial and it follows that there are certain essential qualities that go along with being human. Obviously this does not mean that all human beings are *identical*, merely that they share a certain *essence*, even if that essence takes the form of a *capacity* to be or do something, rather than the physical reality of being or having done something.

Our identity as human beings is not just a word or label attached to us by our culture, but an objective reality, albeit one not fully describable from the subjective point of view in which each of us is confined. We might look at a caterpillar and conclude that its essence relates to its caterpillar-qualities. However, when it turns into a butterfly, its essence would appear to have changed. In fact, objectively, the essence of the creature in question includes all the stages of its existence. This includes its potential, in that the butterfly-quality still forms part of its essence while it is at the caterpillar stage. This remains the case even if it is, for instance, eaten by a bird before it can ever become a butterfly. It does not actually need to *become* a butterfly in order for it to contain the *essence* of butterflyness. As mentioned above, some thinkers have objected to the idea of essential reality on the basis that it defines and restricts the potential of the thing in question. *But that is to confuse an externally-imposed definition or restriction with a quality that is contained within.* The objective essence of a thing, which exists regardless of whether it is ever named or alluded to, is the wholeness of its potential being. Its essence is necessarily broader and higher and deeper than the physical form its existence will take, and so cannot in any way restrict that existence. Instead, *its actual existence will always inevitably be a restriction of the full potential available within its essence.* The actual reality of the existence of the caterpillar eaten by a bird is more limited than the full butterfly-potential which it possesses in its essence.

This limitation which is always implied in a particular existence also applies, of course, to our ultimate essence as an aspect of The Universe. Critics of metaphysical essentialism have therefore missed the point if they imagine that it is the idea of essence *per se* that is a restriction or a limitation. Instead, it is the movement *away* from the ultimate essence towards particular essence and physical form that limits potential. Our ultimate essence is unlimited: it is the *necessary subjectivity* of our existence that constrains us within certain boundaries.

While subjectivity underlies all human experience, it does not represent the *core of our existence.* That core resides, as we have seen, in the objectively-authentic and all-inclusive

Universe. So, while our everyday existence proceeds from a starting point of subjectivity, this cannot be the case on a metaphysical level. There we must start from our essential belonging to The Universe, The Whole, from which all else is a contingent derivation, a temporary blossoming. This metaphysical knowledge or *gnosis* is not necessarily easily achieved. In some ways our belonging to The Universe in this way seems obvious and in other ways unthinkable. Yes, humankind must be a part of The Universe, which must logically be the seat of our ultimate existence. Of course, we cannot really be "independent" or "separate". And yet, there is something disturbing about the idea that humanity is nothing more than a passing and localised form that The Universe has taken. That thought makes us feel even more uneasy when we apply it to our individual existence and see that we are, in turn, merely a tiny part of the human species that is merely a tiny part of The Universe. We *feel* that our own sense-of-life exists within us, comes from within us, so how can we be simply a part of something so much bigger? Rationally, we might understand that although our form is individual, the stuff of which we are made is of humankind, of the planetary organism and of The Universe. But when we focus that understanding on our own selves and conclude that *we* (yes, *you*!) do not actually exist as individuals in the way we think we do, then things become more difficult for us to cope with.

Our primary self-identification as individuals is deeply embedded in contemporary industrial culture and applies even on the social, rather than metaphysical plane. While people may feel some sense of *belonging* to a community, or to the human species, they generally do not regard themselves as being *part* of that broader entity. Indeed, they often react angrily against any such suggestion, since a misunderstanding has developed, in which considering oneself to be a part of a larger entity is seen as a surrender of individuality and freedom. However, as I have argued elsewhere,[9] this stems from a broader misunderstanding of freedom itself, and of the symbiotic relationship that it enjoys with *responsibility*. The individual is not "lost" or "devalued" by being part of a whole, but instead plays the vital role of *representing* the whole, of acting for the whole, of bearing the burden of actual physical existence on the behalf of a more abstract collective entity. A community cannot exist without the individuals that make it up. It is dependent on the individuals that make it up, even though its collective level of existence transcends that of any particular individual. When something is *dependent* on you, the individual, this lends you a weight, a responsibility, which is at the same time your *freedom* to participate in that entity. The assumption of the responsibility of being part of a community or species is the assumption of true individuality. The realisation of individuality is rooted in the acceptance of responsibility, the acceptance of one's own reality and of the need to act on and through that reality.

The same thinking applies on a more abstract level, the "spiritual" one in which an individual becomes aware that the ultimate source of their consciousness lies beyond them, that the prism of individual self-awareness merely refracts the existential "light" of the organic Universe. Also here, people resent the idea that their individual freedom might in some way be compromised by the idea of being part of a greater whole, The Universe. Having seen the way that organised religions have distorted this spiritual understanding into a demand for "obedience" to institutions supposedly representing the separate "God" which they substitute for an all-embracing Universe, they imagine that abandoning the certainty of separate individual existence would also mean abandoning individual validity. Again, this is not so. On the contrary, the importance of the individual as a limited manifestation of the Whole could hardly be greater! Each of us is the whole Universe itself, but condensed and channelled, through necessary subjectivity, into a specific physical form with a specific sense of existence. This is how The Universe actually manifests itself, *exists*, on a real and specific level – through its physical parts, including us.

A possible objection springs to mind: if this metaphysical realisation is so hard to come by, does this not indicate that human beings are not *supposed* to be aware that the separateness of their individual existence is ultimately an illusion? Does that term "necessary subjectivity" not mean, perhaps, that it is *necessary* for us to stay within our subjectivity and to not bother ourselves with ideas of universal wholeness or objective truth which we are not equipped to fully understand? Isn't our role, in fact, dependent on *not* understanding that our ultimate being is universal? Aren't we meant to simply carry on being human beings, in our necessarily subjective way, in the same manner that trees carry on being trees, worms carry on being worms, seagulls carry on being seagulls? In what way would an awareness of the limits of our own subjectivity help us live it out in all its necessity? Wouldn't it, in fact, impede it, get in its way, interfere with the specific role that we have to play within The Universe, the specific responsibilities that we carry?

My answer is that, on the contrary, *to live*

the full potential of a human being necessarily involves an awareness of the limits of our own subjectivity. This is one of the factors that makes us different from other parts of The Universe. Notice that I do not say this makes us in any way "superior" – what meaning can "inferior" or "superior" have when we are talking about the diverse parts of one living thing? Is a bird's beak "superior" to its wings? Are the roots of an oak tree "inferior" to its leaves? Everything has its own nature and it is in the nature of human beings to have the capacity to rise up out of their necessary subjectivity from time to time and take a broader view of existence. How can we know if the same isn't true of other creatures? I can well imagine that the swallow, as well as being very much swallow, is also infused with a sense of being part of the air, the sunshine, the life-system that provides the insects on which it feeds. But human beings have, nevertheless, their own particularly human way of feeling, and thinking, their unity with the Whole. Or at least they have the *capacity* for this feeling. If that capacity is not activated, not realised, this is *not* an instance of a human being merely being human and of going about their human business in a necessarily subjective way, naturally oblivious of any wider picture. Instead, it is an instance of a human being *failing to fulfil their capacity*, their potential, and going about their subjective daily business in a way that would better be described as *less-than-human*, for it in no way reflects the fullness of human essence. A human being who fails to transcend the subjective level of reality is like a caterpillar which never becomes the butterfly that is part of its essence. And the tragedy is made worse by the fact that it is not a hungry bird that thwarts this potential, but a blockage within humankind itself.

There are clear adverse consequences to individuals' lack of a sense of belonging to community or species – a loss of social responsibility, little empathy with others, an absence of community spirit, a general disassociation from the interests of humanity as a whole. In the same way, there are adverse consequences to our unawareness of our consciousness's source in universal rather than individual existence. We lose our connection to nature, for instance, and lose a sense of *meaning* in our existence, a sense of *belonging* to something much bigger than ourselves. We also suffer from the fear of death. We generally assume that our sense of "being alive" is something that is linked to our specific individuality. It miraculously appeared in a puff of existential smoke at the moment of our conception or birth (or at some unspecified point in between – this is never very clear!) and will remain with us until our demise. What happens next is a matter of controversy. Various religious dogmas suggest that this individual sense-of-being continues beyond death. For those within those cultures who find these theories unbelievable, the only alternative seems to be to conclude that there is no further sense-of-being and that the individual is consigned to the void of non-existence. This is a chilling prospect. The idea of not existing at all, not even on the level of non-awareness, the idea that not only will everything that you have ever known, experienced, thought, felt or dreamed no longer exist, but that even the deepest flicker of *you-ness* at your innermost core will have been extinguished, is difficult to take on board.

The absolute nothingness at the heart of this prospect is enough to make you conclude that life, in that context, is nothing other than absurd, a kind of cosmic joke. The gnawing awareness of that ever-approaching oblivion will forever be present in the back of your mind as you live out your life. Perhaps, to escape this shadow of fear, you will plunge yourself into activities that take your mind elsewhere, that distract you from this dreadful "reality". What a way to live! What a negative foundation for an existence! And yet, what an unnecessary burden to carry! There is no need to believe in the simplistic religious notions of life-after-death to escape the horror of the awaiting vacuum. If you can understand that our ultimate essence is in The Universe – that The Universe is a living entity of which are simply a part – then you can understand that your sense-of-being is not tied to your individual existence at all, but pre-dates it and will outlive it. This sense-of-being is the spiritual sap which feeds the branches, twigs and leaves of the tree of universal life. The leaf may fall but the sap still flows. It is this sap which feels, which *is*, inside us. Our necessary subjectivity enables us to function on a day-to-day basis, but it also hides from us, most of the time, our ultimate reality. Our ultimate reality lives on after our individual death and therefore our individual death will not be the absolute void and darkness that we fear, but something more akin to a withdrawal from the specific, a pulling back of the existential focus from the lens of our individual life to the broader view.

It is not so much extinction that awaits us, but diffusion. Diffusion not into darkness, but into the light of the living Universe. Our individual death will not lead to non-being, but to continued being on a level which has always been there, but which maybe has not been a part of our self-definition. When the sun shines and the sky is blue we cannot see the stars. But they are always there. Darkness falls on our particular part of the planet and we are able us to see the vast reality of the cosmos that surrounds us. When the sun has risen again, and the curtain of the sky is once more pulled shut, do we forget that the stars and planets are out there? Do we claim that because we cannot see them, they do not exist? There are those who talk about the being of the individual as the fundamental reality and in saying this they imagine that they are in opposition to the idea of essence. But they are not! Because the being of the individual *is* the being of The Universe. When the individual asserts to themself the reality of their existence, this is The Universe speaking to itself, via the restricted channel of this individual. All being flows from the essence of The Universe. How can it be otherwise if we have defined The Universe as absolutely everything, without exception?

We have arrived back at the two statements cited earlier. *1. It is impossible for us to be completely objective about the truth. 2. There is such a thing as completely objective truth.* There is no contradiction. The subjectivity of individual being, and sense-of-being, is an aspect of the overall objective truth of The Universe. The Universe includes everything. This (obviously) includes us. Therefore our ultimate being and essence are of The Universe. As a consequence, our being does not arise from merely-individual existence and our merely-individual death will not entail the end of that being. Failure to understand the above insight amounts to failure to understand the fundaments of our existence within The Universe. And yet, this lack of understanding is rampant within contemporary culture to the extent that it is those possessing the understanding who are regarded as straying from the norm.

It is worth speculating a little as to why this might be the case, as to why metaphysical attempts to transcend subjectivity – which are sometimes termed "spirituality" – are so often derided. The reasons seem to me to be very complex and to be intertwined with the development of the society in which we currently live. I say "intertwined" because it is not always clear what comes first – the social forces which repress "spiritual" belonging in their own interests or the lack of "spiritual" belonging which allows the interests of these social forces to predominate. A common feature of these reasons also seems to be a form of self-concealment which has enabled them to avoid detection and reversal. For instance, the discrediting of the idea of "spirituality" as I define it – an urge to surpass subjectivity and connect with universal levels of reality – can be partly blamed on religion. The natural soaring of the human spirit, its reaching-out beyond the narrow limits of individual self, is corralled into a different set of narrow limits by religious dogma. There are no greater enemies of true spirituality than organised religions such as the Roman Catholic Church.[10] While movements towards spirituality can occur within religions (Sufism within Islam, for instance) they are often crushed by the forces of religious anti-spirituality. The narrow unspirituality of religion repels people with the greatest sense of *genuine* spirituality. Religion's *claims* to represent spirituality succeed in repelling these people from the very *idea* of spirituality, which would otherwise have attracted them. Things are made even worse by opponents of religion who dismiss spirituality as a disguised form of religion. At the same time, the word "spirituality" is used by other people to describe something that falls short of true spirituality, that is in fact a kind of vapid sentimentality dressed up in quasi-spiritual clothing. The emptying-out from the word "spirituality" of any authentic meaning makes its true essence almost invisible to us. We are not even aware of the potential existence of this authentic spirituality, so how can we be aware that it is something from which we have been largely separated?

Another example of self-concealment by the ideological forces which repress genuine spirituality would be their "official" definition of the universe, discussed earlier. By confining the meaning of "universe" to the physical plane of existence, they block off the possibility of a metaphysical approach, forcing the invention of another term ("The Universe" in this instance) with which to express the real and forbidden content of the word, while not appearing to be doing anything of the sort. A further example can be seen regarding the manifestation of spirituality through a connection to nature, which is a stepping stone between the human level of existence and the awareness of our belonging to The Universe. This spirituality was not only suppressed by the hostility of religion, but by the hostility of an increasingly debased society which saw in the natural world only the means for exploitation and superficial enrichment. But alongside this open antagonism to nature-spirituality gradually came concealed varieties. Because nature was often taken to be brutal and competitive, an attachment to nature was sometimes taken as an endorsement of all that is lowest in humanity, as the opposite of an elevating spirituality. Because sometimes the love of nature, in the face of these trends, later took on an overly sentimental quality, the love of nature was itself taken as sentimental or "unrealistic". The idea that our belonging to nature is both spiritual and real became difficult to find and express amidst all the confusion created by false definitions – and this difficulty itself became a further means by which the idea was lost from view.

Layer upon layer of assumptions has been built over the original loss of authentic spirituality, a whole modern pseudo-philosophical language has been constructed in which it is now impossible to express the banished ideas. And, following the pattern already identified, this denial conceals itself by presenting itself as an advance in thought and those that dissent from its world-view as hopeless relics of a discredited past. The dogma of "progress" dictates that it is considered insane to search for insight in the works of the great philosophers who were writing hundreds or thousands of years ago. All thought must be contained within, and referred back to, a prescribed body of "up-to-date" thinking, whose superiority is apparently ensured merely by the amount of time that separates it from its predecessors. It fits in well with the rejection of all notions of essence and meaning to insist that there are no eternal metaphysical truths that can be rediscovered and re-described by generation after generation and that only propositions derived from theories enjoying contemporary intellectual popularity can be regarded as serious contributions to human thought.

Our understanding of The Universe is

always going to be incomplete. It has to be: we are part of it and necessarily bound to living out our particular part in it, seeing it through individual eyes and occupying a specific physical space. Given the absolute scope of The Universe, we could never in any case hope to come anywhere near describing it. The Universe would not be The Universe if it could be regarded objectively, as an object, from "outside". But our understanding is further obscured, and to an extent that we often do not understand, by the way that our limitations also apply to *time*. If we turn back, for a moment, to the dictionary definition of the universe (without the capital letters), we will recall that it spoke of "all existing matter, energy and space". There is a secondary implication behind the word "existing" here. As well as referring to a physical existence of some kind, it also implies an existence in time, in the present. This has to be so, for otherwise the matter in question would not be seen as "existing" in physical terms either. A dinosaur is not an abstract idea, but a very real and solid animal. However, would it be spoken of as "existing" in current times, except in the shape of fossilised remains? We may say it "exist*ed*" in the past, but the use of this tense shows that we do not regard it as "exist*ing*" now. We appear to limit our definition of "existence" to that which exists at the moment in time in which that definition is being made. What is our justification for this? It would seem to be based on a very clear attachment to the exclusive reality of what we call the "present". But what is this present? Is it something so absolute that it can be used as the foundation stone on which to build our whole conception of what is or isn't real?

In fact, our experience and understanding of time is another aspect of *necessary subjectivity*. The same considerations are at play. The fact that we cannot simultaneously see everything happening in the world does not mean that all those things are not happening, that all those billions of other human lives are less real than our own. We are merely restricted, for practical reasons, to the subjectivity that is part and parcel of our personal existence. We can only live the one life. In terms of time, the fact that we can only live in the present does not mean that the past and future do not exist. How could we live our lives if we did not experience them from a certain vantage point to the exclusion of all others? How could I focus on chopping up a cabbage for my dinner if I could simultaneously see that I hadn't been born yet, the cabbage didn't yet exist and also that I had already eaten it, grown old and died?

The whole of a recorded piece of music is already embedded in the groove of a vinyl record. But we cannot listen to the whole of it at once, in a glorious split-second explosion of sound. Why not? Because the dimension of time is part of the reality of music (and indeed of speech). It needs to exist in time, with temporal extension, in the same way that a sculpture needs to exist in an actual physical space. When the needle follows the vinyl groove it reproduces the music in the dimension in which it makes sense, the dimension of time. Likewise with our lives. The sense of "the present" that keeps us poised between a constantly approaching future and a constantly receding past is like the needle on the record. We need to experience it this way in order to make sense of it all. That doesn't mean that, objectively speaking, the rest of the record or the rest of reality cease to exist. All of that is simply hidden from us by the blinkers of the necessary subjectivity by which we have to lead our lives. We remain aware of the past and the future, of course, in the same way that the enjoyment of the record involves a sense of continuity between what we have just heard and what is still to come. But in our conscious minds we set them aside from the thing we call reality. The past is often very real, but we classify our awareness of it as memories. The future is more obscure, since the needle of our lives has yet to activate it, but its reality is waiting for us.

Instead of imagining The Universe as a massive cosmic blob of matter, energy and space we have to picture a blob that also includes what we think of (from our subjective point of view) as the past and the future. Against any objection that the dimension of "time" cannot reasonably be included in the definition of any "thing", I would point back to the example of music and in addition to films, conversations and football matches. In their full manifestation (rather in terms of a physical disc, transcript or result) they all extend over a temporal dimension and yet their integrity as an identifiable "thing" is not questioned. There is no subjectivity that confines The Universe, there is no restriction to the particularity of one specific viewpoint. It does not merely exist at one point in "time", at one point on the groove of the record. *It is, itself, the whole record rather than the notes we happen to be hearing right now.* It is the whole piece of music, the subjective discovery of which, from our particular perspective, we perceive as the playing of the record, the passing of "time".

This understanding also, incidentally, helps us to grasp the nature of "possibilities", mentioned earlier as abstract realities denied in the purely-physical definition of the universe. Possibilities have to exist before anything can happen. There is the possibility that I will fall off the weir the next time I try to cross the river. If there was no possibility, I wouldn't even need to think about where I put my feet. I could run across with my eyes shut and know that I could never fall off. However, the possibility of me falling into the river is clearly real. It exists. But what happens to that possibility, that real possibility, when it doesn't turn into reality? When I have successfully crossed the river without any accidents, what becomes of the previous possibility of me falling? We can now see that possibilities are not really speculative notions, as they might appear from a subjective viewpoint in time, since they do not in fact refer to things that "might" or "might not" happen in a future yet to be formed. Rather, they are part of the structure by which the "future" – that is to say, the extension of The Universe in the dimension regarded by us as the "future" – takes shape. They form part of the invisible, internal dimensions through which The Universe exists, like magnitude or quantity. As such, they have no actual content in themselves. They are principles, frameworks. The "possibility" of something existing or happening is not a prediction and it is not negated by the eventuality of that thing not coming into being. It is merely the means – neutral and waiting to be activated – by which that thing *could* happen. The possibility of me falling into the water is an abstract pre-condition that has to exist if I am to (possibly) fall. That pre-condition continues to exist regardless of whether or not the reality is fulfilled. If I do not fall, it does not become retrospectively impossible for me to have fallen! That possibility remains, from within the subjectivity of the point before I started to cross the river.

This last point is important, because it is a reminder of the way that possibilities, and thus the "future", remain open from within the subjectivity of a place in "time", regardless of the timeless nature of The Universe. At any particular moment in the subjective reality of "time" we can never be sure of how the process will continue to unfold. The idea that The Universe embraces all time – that from its absolute viewpoint everything is, has and will be happening simultaneously – is worrying for some lovers of human freedom. It seems to imply that there is such a thing as immutable destiny, that the future has already been written and all we can do, as human beings, is live it out with dignity and acceptance. And yet that is not the case at all. *The non-existence of time is only true from the unique viewpoint of The Universe.* It is, and can never, be true from our own necessarily subjective vantage point in the midst of time. Moreover, in the same way that we cannot be objective observers of a Universe of which we are part, we cannot be objective observers of time passing, of "fate" unfolding.

We make our own decisions in life, we steer

our own course. Everything that happens to us in our own lives follows on from a choice we have made. This is not to say that we choose, or deserve, everything that happens to us. We can accidentally find ourselves in the right place, or the wrong place, at the right or wrong time. But we will have arrived there by means of a certain choice we have made at a certain point. It could be countered that the choices we make, blind and inexplicable as they often seem, themselves form part of the "fate" that controls our lives. We are propelled forward, it might be argued, by invisible and irresistible forces that guide us along the path that we were always meant to, that we always had to, follow. From a retrospective personal point of view, of course, that might *appear* to be true. Once a thing has happened, it is fixed and might look as if it had "always" been going to happen. From the alternative perspective of a Universe transcending time, events may also look that way. A process works itself out, lays itself out within the sequence of time, and seems complete in itself. How could it ever have been any different? However, both these imagined perspectives fail to take into account the reality which necessarily conditions our experiences. *They deny the active nature of our present-tense subjectivity.* We do not experience the present as an "observer", casting our mind back from some point in the future and watching what is happening with the full knowledge of how it will all play out. Neither is it somehow possible for us to transcend time altogether, in the way that The Universe does. We are human beings, existing on a physical and temporal plane of reality. We experience the present from the point of view of the present, the stage of the time-process at which it is being shaped. *Our presence-in-the-present empowers us to participate in the process at the only point at which that is possible.* To retrospectively justify our actions on the basis that we were simply going along with what "had" to be, is to hide from our own freedom and our own responsibility, to pretend that somehow we were not "there" in a real present in which our presence was a formative part. It is to deny the important understanding that the future, in the guise of possibilities, remains open from within the subjectivity of our place in time. It is to deny that possibilities have a reality, tied to our time-perspective, and that they necessarily (all "possibilities" are, by definition, possible!) have the potential to turn that abstract reality into a physical one. *Most importantly, it is to deny that we, as human beings present in subjective time, have the power – indeed the responsibility – to help decide whether or not possible reality becomes physical reality.*

Let us take a hypothetical step back for a

moment and ask ourselves why human beings possess this subjectivity-in-time which means we are always riding the crest of the breaking wave of reality as it unfolds. We have seen that it is necessary for our individual daily existence, but is there more to it than that? Here's a related question: as the reality of the Universe unfolds (within the subjectivity of time), how does it shape itself? What are the forces at work that allow it take on the form that it takes? Obviously, it forms *itself* – as it is, by definition, all that there is – but what aspect of itself is involved in the formation? The aspects of The Universe involved in shaping a very time-specific and particular area of reality will be those most relevant to that area. Thus in the world of human affairs, that ongoing self-shaping will naturally be carried out by The Universe by means of human beings. At first glance, that phrase "by means of human beings" might ring alarm bells. Am I saying that, after all, human beings are not free and responsible for their own actions but are merely tools of The Universe? No, because human beings are living parts of The Universe and our freedom and responsibility are, likewise, aspects of The Universe. If an individual anarchist describes themself as part of a broader anarchist movement, this does not mean that they have surrendered their individual freedom and responsibility. Likewise, that broader anarchist movement would not be an anarchist movement without the freedom and responsibility of the individuals out of which it is constituted.

The Universe, in order to be alive, needs living parts. Human beings are among those living parts (and I only focus on human beings on the subjective basis that I am human!). In order to live, in order to form itself, shape itself, it needs those living parts to carry the responsibility appropriate to their sphere of influence. That is why they exist, that is what they essentially *are* – specific and subjectively-functioning organs of the overall whole. The Universe would not be The Universe if it had no actual presence on the physical level of being, if it had no actual presence in the present moment. It needs to *contain the function of subjectivity* in order to be able to be present and to participate in its own self-shaping. We are one of the ways in which The Universe exists on this physical and time-bound plane. We are its representatives, as it were, its avatars in this time and place.

In a metaphorical way, The Universe *descends* into us in order to act through us and through our being. It descends in the sense of passing from an abstract level to a physical one, which is often described as the passing from a "higher" to a "lower" level,[11] but without any sense of inferiority or superiority since we are considering different modes-of-being of one and the same entity. The necessary subjectivity with which we lead our lives is also the necessary subjectivity with which The Universe takes on a real form and becomes both present and active in its own self-shaping. Thus, in a way, we are doubly present in our own subjective experience. Firstly, we are there as our individual selves leading our own individual lives. Secondly, we are there as manifestations of The Universe, of which we all form a living and active part. There is no contradiction between these two forms of presence – they are two aspects of the one reality, two sides of the same coin.

There is a problem when we become too immersed in the one aspect and lose sight of the other. Most commonly, human beings become too attached to the subjective aspect and cling to their individuality at the expense of any larger belonging. But it is also possible to err in the other direction, to retreat from the "illusions" of the physical world and seek reality on a purely spiritual plane. Neither of these is acceptable. We have to be aware of our supra-individual belonging and at the same time understand that we have a duty to use our own individual presence in this world for the benefit of a greater collective interest – whether that be our community, our species, our planet or an intangible sense of *good*. We have to see both sides of the coin at the same time, by setting it spinning perhaps,[12] by living in a state of permanent oscillation between the knowledge that there is an objective truth we can never properly know and the determination to lead our own subjective lives in the *best* way we can. Infused by the *gnosis* of our ultimate belonging to The Universe, our necessary subjectivity is set free to be *real, present and active* at a particular place and at a certain time, to play its part in the self-shaping of history without the crippling fear of individual death – to joyfully accept the full responsibility of authentic human existence.

1. Greil Marcus, *Lipstick Traces: histoire secrète du vingtième siècle* (Paris: Éditions Allia, 1998), p. 276.

2. Plotinus, *The Enneads*, trans. by Stephen MacKenna (London: Penguin, 1991) p. 380.

3. Plotinus, p. 389.

4. Ananda K. Coomaraswamy, *What is Civilisation and Other Essays* (Ipswich: Golgonooza Press, 1989), p. 70.

5. "There is nothing more difficult than to become critically aware of the presuppositions of one's thought". E.F. Schumacher, *A Guide for the Perplexed* (London: Jonathan Cape, 1977), p. 54.

"The individual who has been more deeply marked by this impoverished spectacular thought than by any other aspect of his experience puts himself at the service of the established order right from the start, even though subjectively he may have had quite the opposite intention. He will essentially follow the language of the spectacle, for it is the only one he is familiar with; the one in which he learned to speak. No doubt he would like to be regarded as an enemy of its rhetoric; but he will use its syntax. This is one of the most important aspects of spectacular domination's success". Guy Debord, *Commentaires sur la société du spectacle* (Paris: Gallimard, 1992). p. 38.

6. In *Forms of Freedom* (Sussex: Winter Oak Press, 2015) I use the term "the entity-that-is-not-an-entity" to describe what I am now referring to as The Universe, having encountered the same problem of the general definition of the universe in purely physical terms. It now seems appropriate to me to use the term The Universe for these purposes.

7. Any more than the reality of the sound made by a falling tree depends on someone having heard it – see *2. Denying reality: from nominalism to newthink.*

8. As Plato writes in *Timaeus*: "Suppose a man modelling geometrical shapes of every kind in gold, and constantly remoulding each shape into another. If anyone were to point to one of them and ask what it was, it would be much the safest, if we wanted to tell the truth, to say that it was gold and not to speak of the triangles and other figures as being real things, because they would be changing as we spoke". Plato, *Timaeus and Critias*, trans. by Desmond Lee (London: Penguin, 1977), p. 69.

9. *Forms of Freedom.*

10. See Paul Cudenec, *The Stifled Soul of Humankind* (Sussex: Winter Oak, 2014).

11. See *6. The Eye of the Heart.*

12. See Paul Cudenec, *The Fakir of Florence: A Novel in Three Layers* (Sussex: Winter Oak Press, 2016).

Also from Winter Oak

Paul Cudenec – *The Fakir of Florence: A Novel in Three Layers (2016)*
Paul Cudenec – *Forms of Freedom (2015)*
Paul Cudenec – *The Stifled Soul of Humankind (2104)*
Paul Cudenec – *The Anarchist Revelation: Being What We're Meant to Be (2103)*
Paul Cudenec – *Antibodies, Anarchangels and Other Essays (2013)*
Richard Jefferies – *The Story of My Heart (2015)*
Ed Lord – *Modern Madness: A Wild Schizoanalysis of Mental Distress in the Spaces of Modernity (2016)*
Henry Salt – *Richard Jefferies: His Life and Ideals (2015)*

Full details of all these titles are available on the Winter Oak website at www.winteroak.org.uk, along with our regular anti-capitalist information bulletin The Acorn. To get in touch with Winter Oak please email winteroak@greenmail.net or follow @winteroakpress on Twitter.

Also from Winter Oak

THE ANARCHIST REVELATION

PAUL CUDENEC

Paul Cudenec draws on an impressively wide range of authors to depict a corrupted civilization on the brink of self-destruction and to call for a powerful new philosophy of resistance and renewal. He combines the anarchism of the likes of Gustav Landauer, Michael Bakunin and Herbert Read with the philosophy of René Guénon, Herbert Marcuse and Jean Baudrillard; the existentialism of Karl Jaspers and Colin Wilson; the vision of Carl Jung, Oswald Spengler and Idries Shah, and the environmental insight of Derrick Jensen and Paul Shepard in a work of ideological alchemy fuelled by the ancient universal esoteric beliefs found in Sufism, Taoism and hermeticism.

"The least pessimistic book I can recall reading. It brings anarchist resistance and the spirit together in a very wide-ranging and powerful contribution". John Zerzan, author of *Future Primitive* and *Running on Emptiness*.

Also from Winter Oak

ANTIBODIES, ANARCHANGELS & OTHER ESSAYS

PAUL CUDENEC

Antibodies, Anarchangels and Other Essays brings together a selection of work by Paul Cudenec in which he calls for a new deeper level of resistance to global capitalism – one which is rooted in the collective soul. He leads us along the intertwining environmental and philosophical strands of *Antibodies*, through the passion of *Anarchangels* and *The Task* and on to an informative analysis of Gladio, a state-terrorist branch of what he terms the "plutofascist" system. Also included, alongside short pieces on Taoism and Jungian psychology, is an interview with the author, in which he explains key aspects of his approach.

"Very readable and profoundly thoughtful... Many new insights on the destructive relationship between the greater part of humanity and the planet which tries to sustain them". Peter Marshall, author of *Demanding the Impossible: A History of Anarchism.*

Also from Winter Oak

THE STIFLED SOUL OF HUMANKIND

PAUL CUDENEC

Paul Cudenec depicts a humanity dispossessed, a society in which freedom, autonomy, creativity, culture, and the spirit of collective solidarity have been deliberately suffocated by a ruthlessly violent and exploitative elite. But he also identifies an underground current of heresy and resistance which resurfaces at key moments in history and which, he argues, has the primal strength to carry us forward to a future of vitality and renewal.

"We have to reintroduce ourselves to history, not as observers but as participants. The power that we can rediscover in ourselves is, among other things, the power to create the future. Prophecy brings hope, hope brings courage, courage brings action, action brings inspiration, inspiration brings more determination, renewed hope, deepened courage. Once this magical spiral of revolt has started spinning, it takes on a life of its own".

Also from Winter Oak

RICHARD JEFFERIES: HIS LIFE AND HIS IDEALS

HENRY S. SALT

"He was a pagan, a pantheist, a worshipper of earth and sea, and of the great sun 'burning in the heaven'; he yearned for a free, natural, fearless life of physical health and spiritual exaltation, and for a death in harmony with the life that preceded it".

So is the writer Richard Jefferies (1848-1887) described by Henry S. Salt in this study first published in 1894. The book sparked controversy at the time, as Salt – a campaigner for animal rights, vegetarianism and socialism – used it to claim Jefferies for one of his own, highlighting the social radicalism and nature-based spirituality in his subject's later writing. He demolishes the conservative presentation of Jefferies as a mere chronicler of country life and reveals him as a flawed yet inspirational figure whose best works were "unsurpassed as prose poems by anything which the English language contains". With a preface by Paul Cudenec.

Also from Winter Oak

THE STORY OF MY HEART

RICHARD JEFFERIES

"Having drunk deeply of the heaven above and felt the most glorious beauty of the day, and remembering the old, old, sea, which (as it seemed to me) was but just yonder at the edge, I now became lost, and absorbed into the being or existence of the universe. I felt down deep into the earth under, and high above into the sky, and farther still to the sun and stars. Still farther beyond the stars into the hollow of space, and losing thus my separateness of being came to seem like a part of the whole".

Richard Jefferies' masterpiece of prose-poetry expresses his sublime yearning not just for connection with nature but for spiritual transcendence. This new Winter Oak edition includes a preface by writer Paul Cudenec exploring the significance of Jefferies' work against a backdrop of disillusionment with industrial civilization and a cultural urge for the regeneration of human society.